A PRAYER AS A POEM FOR EACH DAY

EXPRESSING HOPE THAT EACH AND EVERY DAY

BY
RICHARD A. DIXON

Copyright © 2008 by Richard A. Dixon

A Prayer As A Poem For Each Day
Expressing Hope That Each and Every Day
by Richard A. Dixon

Printed in the United States of America

ISBN 978-1-60477-646-1

All rights reserved solely by the author. The author guarantees all contents are original and do not infringe upon the legal rights of any other person or work. No part of this book may be reproduced in any form without the permission of the author. The views expressed in this book are not necessarily those of the publisher.

Unless otherwise indicated, Bible quotations are taken from the King James Version, Giant Print Edition. Copyright © 1990 by NELSON, A Regency Bible from Thomas Nelson, Inc.

www.xulonpress.com

ACKNOWLEGEMENT

A very special acknowledgement to my former co-worker
and friend, Donna Barrie for assisting
me in editing this book and her unending encouragement
to inspire me to continue my endeavor to write,
and to her husband, Philip, for his understanding in
sacrificing her time that could have been used
as quality family time. Also, many
thanks to her sister, Amber Booker,
for her technical assistance.

DEDICATION

I dedicate this inspirational book of poems to
all of those
who endeavor to write His Word.

As it is written, "Psalm 68:11
The LORD gave the WORD: great was the company of
those
that published it".

PREFACE

The title, "A PRAYER AS A POEM FOR EACH DAY, EXPRESSING HOPE THAT EACH AND EVERYDAY", denotes that 24 hours in which we should focus. Concentrating on one day at a time. We should only relate to yesterday by learning from it and responding to it positively and by doing so, relate to tomorrow as being better than today.

Each day we search for that additional something that will lift us in spirit and give us hope for each day. Although we get down on our knees and pray each day to ignite our spiritual spark, but as humans we need more soul-searching power in between to give us more inspiration to assist us in meditating and communicating with our God. By diligently reading these meaningful compact inspirational poems during your selected time of the day, you will find them powerful and a simplicity in their spiritual meaning. This within itself makes them understandable to the not so poetic mind.

These poems are written to stimulate you spiritual mind as guidelines that will lead you in the direction of giving you hope and to fortify your faith. The reference bible verses at the end of the poems relates to the content of the poems.

A Prayer As A Poem For Each Day

The Bible
Verses were purposely not completed as written in the Bible so that it will influence you, the reader, to go to your Bible and open it, to receive the full message of the designated chapter and verse.

We need to find and maximize our effectiveness to do the right thing and we must find our place in the stream of goodness and the purpose of the universe. Read these poems with your heart in search for that good and spiritual life.

THE ORIGINAL SEVEN DAYS

It was written, "For GOD Saw It Was Good", in many instances to describe his creation. If we can just relate and connect to everything that he did during his creation, we will come to understand that we are actively connecting to his glorious lifeline.

The Original First day

On this first day of all days let us pray and look at the
creation of earth beginning where there was
no form and no void.
There was total darkness but then on that first day
GOD brought light from out of
that empty tabloid.
Let us pray and relate to this first day and concentrate
on bringing our lives out of the dark where we find
the pits of the night.
Let us pray and start to remember that GOD gave us the
day to rejoice and bring our lives to live in the
splendor of the light.

The Original Second Day

Let us pray on the second day of the creation and come
to the reality there is a glorious Heaven
and then there is earth.
For GOD on that second day of His creation made the
firmament and at that moment his glorious heaven
made it divine birth.
Let us pray that heaven should always be in
our hearts so that we can all live in
this world with love.

On this day give your life a chance to remember that
we all can live that eternal life in that
glorious heaven above.

The Original Third Day

Let us pray and be thankful that on the third day we
were blessed because God's creation of water
and land came to be.
By his wish or the word of God for us, land was created
and called earth and the creation of the
water was called the sea.
Also on this day let us give thanks for the creation of
grass, plants, fruit and trees and their yielding
seeds to reproduce in number.
Let us all allow the seeds within all of us to bear the fruit
that God desires and let us be thankful
and never slumber.
Let us all pray and show our gratitude to God for
giving us an environment and with our
efforts we can live.
Let us walk this land as proud children of God and utilize
the sea and let us share and care and show our
love when we give.

The Original Fourth Day

On this day, God wanted definite integrals of time
between the light and darkness to divide
the night from the day.
The light created in his firmament in heaven made the
divides along with the signs for all seasons,
days, years in every way
With this creation we have been given a monitor to
formulate our calendars and to show us time
and its earthly insight.
We are thankful that we can somewhat measure our
duration because the greater light rules the day and the
lesser rules the night.
We must not forget what was God's response, when
He created our full day and night, and God saw
and said, "It was good".
Let us pray that under the creation of the sun, moon,
and stars, we will follow His word both day
and night, as we should.

The Original Fifth Day

Let us give thanks for the God's fifth day of creation for
His wish was that the water brings forth-moving
creatures and foul that fly above.
God's wish that all creatures will multiply its kind, both the
ones in the water and the winged fowl and this was the
birth of our loving dove.
The wonders and purpose of these creatures have
given us as mankind a way to live our lives
and with this we should give thanks.
God knew what His master plan would be for us and
we should show that thanks when we see that fowl
and when we approach a riverbank.

The Original Sixth Day

Let us pray and give thanks for on the sixth day
God said, "let the earth bring forth
the living creatures of its kind".
After God made the cattle, creeping things, and beast,
man was made in His image and this was
good and well defined.
And God said, "let man have dominion over all
other creatures on the land and in the sky
and in the sea".
When God created man in his own image, we all became
His children and this became known to us as
his personal decree.

We should pray always to try to conceive the majestic of God's creation and never doubt how
mighty he is and always been.
We should always show our gratitude by doing our
part by help saving this earth that He created
from torment and sin.

The Original Seventh Day

Let us all pray for on the seventh day God ended
His work of creations and He rested from
all of his wonderful actions.
His creations have been put into place to give us a
earthly life that will assist us in leading
us to positive factions.

At times, let us take a day and rest from the worldly
things of life, that material world and
redirect our search.
Let us concentrate on the sharing and caring,
the spiritual things of life, the good-
ness and purpose of the universe.
Let us pray to balance our material and spiritual
world for we could have heaven on earth and
this will be our glorious assess.
Let us pray and walk by His side and assist our
LORD by working with his master plan
so that we will be daily blessed.

A Prayer As A Poem — Richard A. Dixon

January 1

Thanking the Almighty for This New Year

On this day I pray and give thanks
to my God for bringing us
into this New Year.
I pray for a better life for my family and
to all especially whom are close
and are very dear.
I pray that our plans will be first to put
love, honesty and unselfishness in
all of our affairs,
so that our resolutions will be founded on good
values and our spirituality
will be unimpaired.
I pray that sharing and caring and all of the
love things will be the goals
that we fulfill.
I pray that all that who are believers can
have that better year in climbing
that spiritual hill.

Corinthians 15:57
But thanks be to God which give us victory———

Isaiah 61:2
To proclaim the acceptable year of the LORD———

A Prayer As A Poem — Richard A. Dixon

A Prayer As A Poem For Each Day

January 2

The Right Voice for the Right Things

I pray on this day that I will be an improved person,
come this new year, for it would be negative
to get stuck in last year's mode.
With this necessary change it demands diligent
actions, by stop putting things off and stay
on that positive road.
Anything worth doing can succeed by being pure
in heart, for our heart tells you
the right things to do,
That do-nothing negative voice keeps me in a hole
and my life goes nowhere and these things
will certainly come true.
I pray to know that it doesn't matter whether I am
down on my knees or standing, or walking, for it
is from my heart in what I say.
I pray always to listen to only the Almighty's voice
that comes from within, and what He tells
me I will follow without any delay.

Revelation 3:20
Behold I stand at the door and if any man hear my voice,
I will Come to him———

A Prayer As A Poem—Richard A. Dixon

January 3

Be Inspired To Face Reality

Let me pray on this day to find that spiritual
motivation to inspire me to do the
positive things in life.
I pray to check my priorities and to get them
right for I might be aspiring for the things
that bring me strife.
I pray first to pray each and every day to be in-
spired by doing the will of God everyday in
everything that I do.
I should ask my LORD to balance my aspirations with
the world's so I may find joy in
my career's breakthroughs.
I pray that I will always understand that this earth
is our testing ground and our stay here
is strictly temporarily.
I pray never to forget from whence I came which
is our Almighty who will spiritually
give us eternity.

Timothy 3:16
All scriptures are given by the inspiration of God
And is profitable———

Revelation 21:1
For the first heaven and the first earth passed away
And there was no more sea-

A Prayer As A Poem—Richard A. Dixon

January 4

Honesty And Being Pure In Heart

I pray on this day to have a genuine happy
life here on earth but honesty is one
thing I can't leave out.
For honesty is a necessity to be with God and
to be pure in heart with him is exactly
what it's all about.
When you know that you are right with the
Almighty calmness and serenity becomes
second nature to your heart,
You become at peace with yourself in your daily
affairs, and in your heart happiness becomes
an intricate part.
I pray never to think that I am mighty enough to
handle this world and all of the trouble
that I may face.
I pray to be spiritual smart and give my life
a real chance by living off of the
Almighty Amazing Grace.

Romans 13:13
Let us all walk honesty as in the day———
Not in stripe and envying———

A Prayer As A Poem — Richard A. Dixon

January 5

Work with GOD

On this day I pray that if I find myself without
doing anything and I find myself
without work,
I pray to understand that an idle mind is the devil's
workshop and to work with God should
be my search.
I pray that at this time I should fill my mind with
his words for this will prevent my
spirit not to corrode.
By working with God and following his guidelines,
good things happen and I can save myself
from that sinful byroad.
I pray by working with the Almighty, His light will
appear in my darkest night and I will see
what faith can bring,
I pray and know that the sadness and the burdens
will fall from me and my heart and soul will
forever rejoice and sing.

John 9:4I
must work the works of Him that sent me, while it is still day———

A Prayer As A Poem — Richard A. Dixon

January 6

On Heavenly Grounds

On this day I pray to keep it on the road, on
the path that will spiritually protect and
guide us to the eternal beyond.
I pray that we all will venture that strip of
glorious land with Its biblical markings like
Matthew, Mark, Luke, and John.
GOD gave us this road, this path for all to see and so
that we can get closer by walking toward him
on his special sacred terrain.
It gives us a chance to experience heaven on earth,
it gives us a chance to carry his banner as a believer
in his glorious campaign.
Although the going might get tough the thought
of the final destination will push us
and make us spiritually sound.
I pray that we will all open our hearts to God and
see that path with its lighted sign indicating that
this is God's Heavenly Grounds.

Psalm 16:11
He will show me the path of life; in this presence is the fullness of joy———

A Prayer As A Poem — Richard A. Dixon

January 7

Giving Always To Others

On this day I pray that whomever I meet or
make contact with, will be blessed by
my LORD above.
I pray to be able to influence that person by having me to make their day and I gave their
heart a godly shove.
Yes, I pray at all time that I will walk in the
footsteps that My LORD has
prepared for me.
On this day and forever more let me do all good
things and pray that he will make
my soul sin-free.
Reaching out at all times, even if they do not
welcome my help because of
their negative pride.
Yes, I pray to let them know that I am always
in prayer for them and I will always
stand by their side.

2Corinthians 9:7
According to every man and his purpose in his heart, so let him give———

A Prayer As A Poem — Richard A. Dixon

January 8

The Blessings-His Gift

I pray on this day that I will never forget
that I am indeed blessed because of
my spiritual aims.
At this very moment I am blessed because of my
spiritual connection that has been
heavenly ordained.
The reason why these glorious gifts have been given
to me for I have opened my heart up to
my merciful Almighty.
By coming to him with my heart honest and true,
His doors of heaven are open
to me for eternity.
I pray today that all of my sisters and brothers
will realize that they are also blessed and they
can receive even more,
By remaining strong to that ultimate commitment
to Him and by opening wide
their heart's selfish door.

James 1:7
Every good gift and every perfect gift is from above——

Psalm 103:2
Bless the LORD, my soul, and forget not all his benefits———

A Prayer As A Poem—Richard A. Dixon

January 9

He will Lift and Uphold Me

On this day I pray that my God will uphold
me whenever my frailties jump up and
cause me to fall.
I pray that he will see me through the
bad days and He will help me
with my heavy haul.
In this oscillating world when dreams are
broken and everything seems
to go wrong,
I pray that I will follow my spiritual heart,
because by doing this, my faith
will remain strong.
I pray that at these times that I will
find complete safety in the
spirit of his word,
I know that he will pick me up and make my way,
for him to forsake me at this
time will be absurd.
As long as we all are on the face of this
earth we will completely
fall or stumble,
But our LORD will always rescue us and I
pray that we will show our thanks by
being eternal humble.

Psalm 145:14
The LORD will uphold all that fall———

A Prayer As A Poem — Richard A. Dixon

January 10

Be Spiritual First Not Worldly

On this day I pray to be spiritual first not world-
ly, I pray to loosen my grip on what
the world only has to give.
I pray and believe that all should strive to be
spiritual in His name, that the
way that we should live.
I pray not to lose myself in seeking
only the temporary treasures
of this earth,
I pray that I will be only directed or guided
by his ways to find those eternal
things of worth.
The right road to follow is to balance your life
by receiving these earthly
things through him.
We must understand that nothing has
any real value, if it comes through
the act of sin.
I pray to enjoy life as it should be enjoyed
by allowing my spiritual priority
to be my guide.
I pray to know that we can find heaven on
earth, by putting Him first and
walk by his side.

Isaiah 11:2
And the spirit of the LORD shall rest upon him———
The spirit of the knowledge and of the fear of the
LORD.

A Prayer As A Poem—Richard A. Dixon

January 11

GOD will see us through the Day Or Night

On this day I pray that I will find myself to be
able to see some of what my
purpose in life reveals.
I pray to hear what my LORD says to me for
I will make sure that my heart is
to him, will not be sealed.
I pray that we will all open up our hearts completely to him that we can hear the
words that tells us what's right.
I pray that we will all opens up our hearts
so that we can see the radiance
of his heavenly light.
We should continue to pray for sometimes we
get lost in the dark and we can not see
the right things to do,
Let us recognize that our LORD works as well in
the dark as the light, therefore at anytime
He will see us through.

Philippians 4:4
Always rejoice in the LORD; and again———

A Prayer As A Poem — Richard A. Dixon

A Prayer As A Poem For Each Day

January 12

Stand Tall As A Believer

On this day I pray to stand still and tall as a be-
liever although I may be labeled as
being odd in my way of living.
I pray not to join in with others in gossiping
and hate, I will be different by being
understanding in my giving.
I pray to mode my self-control in the ways
of kindness to make sure that I will
find God's happiness.
I pray not to follow others down that road that
leads to torment Just because there is
someone they want to impress.
I pray to think things through and to say, and
to do the things that my God
would want me to do.
Although today I stand alone, but maybe soon
the others will come and walk with me in
his path to help us all to endure.

Exodus 14:13
And Moses said to the people fear not and stand still
And see the salvation of the LORD———

A Prayer As A Poem — Richard A. Dixon

January 13

Balance Your Life with His Spirit

On this day I pray to balance my life by taking
myself out of the center of focusing on
myself day and night.
I pray that the center of my life will be filled
with his spirit so that I can carry
on his spiritual fight.
I pray that God will intervene and guide me in His
glorious ways, for right things through him
can be obtained.
I pray that we will conceive His values and to
understand that everything from Him is forever
personally ordained.
I pray to take myself out of the spotlight for
it will give me a clearer mind to
focus on others.
I pray that I will find ways of helping my
neighbors and passing His spirit on
from one to another.
I pray to remember that if we want to
balance our lives and live
them effectively,
We need to place God first in the center of our
world so that we will be in
harmony collectively.

Philippians 2:4
Man should not be just concerned about his own things
but also the things of others———

A Prayer As A Poem — Richard A. Dixon

January 14

Feel the Pain of Others

On this day I pray that I will feel the pain of others
although I may not know them or
know where they live.
I pray that I will render them service although
my help is not welcomed at
the time that I give.
I pray that I will always be able to feel the
pain and all of the evil that goes
with their misery.
I pray that I will continue to show my com
passion no matter what the
problem may be.
Giving all to others what God has given to me,
being that channel for his spirit to
flow from me to all freely.
I pray to be that emissary to help ease the pain,
and to show others how to live with
God and to live earnestly.

Proverbs 25:21
If your enemy be hunger give him bread to eat, and if he is thirty———

Galatian 6:2
You should bear one another's burdens, and fulfill the law———

A Prayer As A Poem—Richard A. Dixon

January 15

Finding Peace

On this day I pray to throw those things out of my
mind that bother me for they only
harbor negative fears.
I will replace them with spiritual values to
obtain my supply of joy and my
abundance of cheers.
I pray to give my life a chance to live in peace
with Him so that happiness and
love will never cease.
I will invite my God's love into my heart for I
know I will find only goodness as I
enjoy His eternal lease.
I will release myself from the binds of the world
and hold them loosely for they
bring lingering stress.
I pray to attach myself to the eternal things
of heaven that will guide me through
his maze of happiness.

John 14:27
I leave you my peace I give to you; Not as the world gives———

A Prayer As A Poem — Richard A. Dixon

January 16

Connecting and Cooperating with My LORD

On this day I pray that all of my days will be
a part of that chain that join us in
that spiritual connection.
I pray that my thoughts will become com-
pletely aware of my God and
His glorious perfection.
For it is when I have this consciousness
of my almighty submerged deep
in my heart.
I am at my best, my world is filled with joy
and serenity my life is a heavenly
spirit of art.
I pray by forming this connection with
my LORD, my horizons will extend
far, far beyond,
I know that my love, and knowledge of the
world will become real because of this
God made bond.

Matthew 18:20
For when two or three gathered, together in my name—

A Prayer As A Poem—Richard A. Dixon

January 17

The Goodness That God gives

On this day I pray to allow my heart to be awakened
by the manifestation of the goodness
that only God can give.
I pray that every word come directly from Him and
that my every thought be only the thoughts
that God lives.
I pray that it will forever become known in
my heart that all that is good only come
from His heavenly bin.
I pray that I will be that channel to pass this
goodness to all that I meet to fight the
torment of sin.
Again I pray that my efforts will be that spi-
ritual force that will help us all come
together in one accord,
and may we all become totally aware by doing
his work of goodness, we all will receive
his glorious reward.

Psalm 23:6
Surely goodness and mercy shall follow me all the days
of my life———

A Prayer As A Poem — Richard A. Dixon

January 18

Practice And Grow everyday

On this day I pray that I will continue to develop
my spiritual skills by consistently exercising
my mind with spiritual practice.
I pray that I will be that better person today
than I was yesterday by following my
daily religious tactics.
I pray that I must forever understand that I
should always keep the spirit of God's
awareness in my mind,
For it is through the spirit that I will continue
to grow as the flower grows in the
season of springtime.
I pray that I will never allow my mind to
be idle and allow the devil's
workshop to enter it.
I pray that I will always occupy my heart and
soul with love and to these I
will forever commit.

2Peter 3:18
But grow in grace, and in the knowledge of The Lord and
Savior Jesus Christ———

A Prayer As A Poem — Richard A. Dixon

January 19

Place God At The Center Of Your Life

On this day I pray not only for myself to
follow the will of my God as
the days evolve,
I pray for all mankind to be guided by his
spirit to make sure that good
will be the resolve.
For I believe that in praying for each other,
we will somehow become closer as He
wills us to do.
That is the reason why God should be the center
of all things in our world when
the day is through.
I pray that sharing and caring will be my
way as I travel through
the trials of the day,
I pray by doing these virtues, I will be an
instrument for God to show others
this is His loving way.

1.John 1:7
But if we walk in the light, as he is in the light, we have fellowship with one another———

A Prayer As A Poem — Richard A. Dixon

January 20

Imagine the Eternal

On this day I pray that I will always keep those
Godly thoughts in my mind, all of the Godly
things that I believe.
To think eternal may be a bit out of my thought
process, for this is only God's dimension and
only he can conceive.
I pray and thank God for giving us His grace and
the mere thought of putting us
in His master plan.
This expectation inspires my very soul and motivates my actions to make sure my hand is
always in His hand.
I pray that I will not be bothered because I can not
even come close to describing or understanding
the meaning of eternal life.
I pray just to continue to keep the faith and trust in
Him, so that I will be motivated to keep walking
toward his heavenly site.

Roman 6:23
For the wages of sin is death, but the gift of God is eternal life through Jesus Christ———

A Prayer As A Poem — Richard A. Dixon

January 21

Daily Filling My Heart with Love

On this day I pray to start this day by putting
love in my heart to all that I make contact
with and meet.
I pray that by reaching out to all will
become a daily pattern to make my
day complete.
I pray that my loving heart will always
somehow touch other hearts as I
travel on my way.
I pray that in return the heart that I touch will
in return make someone else's time
a blessed day.
I pray that somehow in this prayer that most of
us will come to understand the power
of a loving heart,
For a smiling face, a helping hand could
bring us together by giving each that
welcomed jump start.

John 4:7
Let us love one another, for love is of God———

A Prayer As A Poem — Richard A. Dixon

January 22

Making Time To Spend Quality Time with God

On this day I pray to set aside time for God and
to make this day as an example of how
I would want all of my days to be.
By spending this quality time with my
LORD there will be nothing but
good that I will only see.
For His namesake let me not just depend
on others to pray for me each time
that I go to church.
At times, I must speak to my God personally
and get down on my knees and do my
own spiritual search.
Let me remember to pray daily and ask
Him to forgive me and to protect
me from sin,
For I must be accountable and ask my
LORD for that forgiveness when
I come to Him.

Psalm 34:4
I sought the LORD and he heard me and he delivered me from all———
A Prayer As A Poem — Richard A. Dixon

January 23

Praying Is God Given

On this day I pray to remind myself that whenever
I pray I gain strength and enlightenment
for my whole being.
Each time that I pray my whole self become glo-
rified like a spiritual awareness carried
on the power of an angel's wing
Praying is not just a ritual that you methodically
go through forming a habit on things
you say from day to day.
For praying is a God given virtue that only
the pure in heart can reach other
hearts in what they say.
You find that real praying gives you a conscious-
ness of God and you can feel His
spirit is deeply within you.
Your whole self becomes a spiritual bond in
this communion with Him for the
things that you say are true.
I pray that in all of my encounters with my
God in prayer my life will become
better than before.
I pray that in my praying my character
becomes stronger, and my heart will
be consistently restored.

Job 22:27
You shall make your prayer unto him, and he Shall hear thee———

A Prayer As A Poem — Richard A. Dixon

January 24

My Quiet Time with Him

On this day I pray that I will always set aside
quiet time to be with my God, the Father,
the Son, the Holy Ghost.
I pray that my daily actions and His way will
not be taken lightly, but continue to
be my guiding post.
I pray that my quiet time will inspire the rest
of my day and give me strength and
guidance to do His will.
Let me be totally attentive during this quality time
by Blocking out all negatives, and making
my being totally still.
I pray that I will become completely conscious of
my Almighty so that I will be aware of every
thing that happens that day.
I pray that I will be able to pass all that He
gives to me to all others, so that we can pro-
tect ourselves from going astray.

Psalm 59:17
Evening and morning and at noon, I will pray———

A Prayer As A Poem — Richard A. Dixon

January 25

To Understand, Continue to Pray

On this day I pray to continue to understand
that when I pray with my heart, every single
word is heard by God above.
By employing my will to do His will, my prayer
becomes a channel to spread love like the
olive leaf carried by the dove.
So I pray that all others will understand
the meaning and what the power
of prayer can do.
For in praying all will find that happiness can be
found here on earth and it is for all and
not just for the few.
So everyday let me not forget that I am continuously building a bond for all
that is good when I pray.
I pray that we know that this is God's purpose to love one another with his
spirit every given day.

Acts 6:4
We will give ourselves continually to prayer———

A Prayer As A Poem — Richard A. Dixon

January 26

With My Daily Spiritual Strength

On this day I pray to find that spiritual
direction to guide me to walk on that
righteous path.
I pray that my spiritual efforts will give me
strength and take me from that
world of wrath.
I pray that through my loving efforts and
as I travel I will be able to
share this love,
and that I will always serve as His way to
pass His good that comes
directly from above.
In this prayer may I be able to gain even more
strength to carry on with
my spiritual skills,
Allowing me to give a helping hand when help
is needed for this is fulfilling
His eternal will.

2Samuel 22:33
God is my strength and power: and He makes my way———
    A Prayer As A Poem — Richard A. Dixon

January 27

Let Us Show Gratitude

On this day I pray that I will show my gratitude
to my Almighty for this day that
He has given all of us.
I woke up this morning breathing the air,
watching the sun rise and through Him
this is a heavenly plus.
Through His grace He has brought us through
lots of trials and tribulation that
only He can do,
and He keeps reminding us through His spiritual
signs that he loves us and He wants to share
all with me and you.
So I pray today that I will forever strive to put
all of His wills and all of His ways
in all of my affaires.
And I pray that I will not only say these words
as a daily habit but I will do this and put
them in all of my prayers.

Psalm 92:1
It is a good thing to give thank unto the LORD———

A Prayer As A Poem—Richard A. Dixon

January 28

Wait and Put It in His Hands

On this day I pray that I will not go too far
in trying to take up or trying to solve the
problems of others.
I pray to recognize the right thing to do is to
put the problem in His hands to care
for my sisters and brothers.
I pray that I will come to the understanding
that I need to be lead by the
hand of my LORD,
For it is only through Him and by Him that
we can find the wisdom to obtain
that spiritual reward.
For it will be wrong for me alone to rush
into a situation and to employ idle
or negative chatter.
I will pray for that calmness and wait to be
guided by God to solve complex
personal matters.

Psalm 28:14
Wait on the LORD: be of good courage, and He shall strengthen thine heart:———

A Prayer As A Poem — Richard A. Dixon

January 29

Putting Your Priorities in Place

On this day I pray that I will consistently
understand, and that is, to make sure
that I put God's will and way first.
For it is only through the almighty that things
are eternal and It is only His way that
will satisfy our spiritual thirst.
Putting material things as your primary goals
should never be the direction in
which you go.
In this process real permanent values will be
for naught, for they did not come in with
His spiritual flow.
We cannot have love for God and a similar
love for material things that are
of this earth.
I pray that we walk with the wisdom of the
Almighty, to balance the world and gain
its spiritual worth.

Proverbs 4:7
Wisdom is the principal thing: therefore to get Wisdom–
——get understanding—

A Prayer As A Poem — Richard A. Dixon

January 30

Strive to Preserve and Keep His Love In Your Heart

On this day I pray that I will continue to
maintain that glorious thought
to preservere.
I pray to strive with the strength that heaven
can give to shield me from all that
earthly fear.
There were times I made mistakes and did
not put my problems into the safety of
my Almighty's hand.
It was then that everything went wrong,
torment was my friend and I walked
on the devil's land.
Now I pray that I will put just as much energy in
my current spiritual life as when I played that
mixed-up mind part,
I pray that I will always remember to persevere and
sustain the efforts to keep this love that He has
placed so gently in my heart.

Jeremiah 31:3
The LORD hath appeared of old unto me, saying, Yea, I
Have loved thee with an everlasting love:———

A Prayer As A Poem — Richard A. Dixon

January 31

Keeping That Selfishness under Control by Thinking of Others

I pray on this day that I will put it in my mind
to think of others in doing a
deed for good.
I pray that I will put my selfishness out of my
mind and follow God's lead and do the
things I should.
I pray that God will continue to manage my selfish
ways for it appears at the most
inopportune time,
For no explained reason, it can jump out of my head
and cause all sort of trouble and turn good
into a grind.
Although we can not explain ourselves completely
about that self that lives deep
inside of us,
I pray that with His spirit in my heart, I will be able
to conquer it and make this day a
brotherhood plus.

1John 2:10
He that love his brother abides in the light———

A Prayer As A Poem — Richard A. Dixon

A Prayer As A Poem For Each Day

February 1

Walk, Talk, And Listen To Him

I pray on this day that I will go through this
day walking with my God and
being unafraid.
When I walk, I pray that I will feel His
presence in my every step of that
spiritual promenade.
I pray that I will not be remiss in our
joyous walk, but talk to Him as we
travel along the way.
He is always available to talk, to pass His
word on to us no matter what come,
no matter what may.
I pray that also on this day that my heart
and soul will be ready and open to listen
for His every word.
But most of all, I pray that I will be aware
and respond positively in what He said
and what I heard.
I pray that I will make it a daily rule to
walk, talk, and listen to my God and
in Him I will abide.
Let me be a prime example to all for it
is indeed a glorious privilege to walk
with Him by His side.

2 Corinthians 5:7
For we walk by faith and not by———

A Prayer As A Poem — Richard A. Dixon

February 2

Learning From Mistakes To Live Right

On this day I pray to show my gratitude for
His grace and giving me this day, I will
strive to do His every will.
I will respond to my mistakes of yesterday spirit-
ually only to develop and to improve
upon my spiritual skills.
I pray that I will only think of tomorrow by
remembering all of the positives that I
can carry into that day.
I pray that I will live right this twenty-four
hours in every sense of the word goodness
and to this I will not stray.
It is written that we can only handle one day
at a time, anything more could
cause a terrible plight.
I pray that I will let all yesterdays and tomor-
rows take care of themselves, but for today
I will strive to get it right.

Proverbs 27:1
Boast not thyself of tomorrow for you know not what a day may———

A Prayer As A Poem — Richard A. Dixon

February 3

Forgiving Your Fellowman

I pray on this day to begin it with love in my
heart for all whom that I have felt have
done me wrong.
I amend this prayer of this forgiveness and pray
that we all will come together in singing
His spiritual songs.
I pray that I will always continue to forgive and
to pray to be aware that God forgives
me everyday.
It is written that we should forgive others seventy
times seven no matter what they may
do or say.
Caring and sharing for all our fellowman
should be our principals and should
always be preserved.
I pray that I will never forget that my God
has forgiven me more than
I ever deserved.

Matthew 6:12
And forgive us our debts; as we forgive our———

Matthew 6:14
For when you forgive men their trespasses, your
Heavenly father will also———

A Prayer As A Poem — Richard A. Dixon

February 4

Doing Better

On this day I pray that I will not live just on
the positive things that I
did yesterday.
I pray that I will regard this day as my opportunity to do good in every
single way.
And in this prayer, I pray that I will include
others and inspire them to do what is
right for all.
For when we pray together, we will stay together and bring down that menacing
evil wall.
From experience, I know that it is dangerous
not to progress from day to day and to say
I can do no more.
So, I make it a special point to pray that I
will indeed do better than I did
the day before.

2 Peter 3:18
But grow in grace, and in the knowledge of the Lord and Savoir———

A Prayer As A Poem — Richard A. Dixon

February 5

Anger Is Not The Way

I pray on this day that I will not employ anger
that serves no one when responding to
most things in life.
From proven experiences it has been
concluded that the results end in
some negative stripe.
It has also been found that these harsh approaches
will sometimes tarnish your mind in
a negative way.
I pray that no one becomes a slave to misery
and to allow their peace of mind to go
completely astray.
I pray that God will give me the strength to
fight the demons that causes anger to
raise its ugly head.
On this day I will pass God's finish line with peace
of mind by committing to be one of His
spiritual thoroughbreds.

Proverbs 15:1
A soft answer turn away wrath: grievous words stir up———

A Prayer As A Poem — Richard A. Dixon

February 6

Seeking The Kingdom Of Heaven

On this day I pray to continue to seek the king
dom of heaven and I pray that this prayer will
bring me closer to my goal.
I pray that this earnest prayer will show others
that these are standards that God
helps me to uphold.
I pray that all will see that to pray with honesty
first in your heart gives you guidelines in
striving to do what's right.
It is my prayer that all people will someday find
the answers in their search which is now out of
their reach and sight.
I pray that all will continue to seek the kingdom of
heaven for that's the goodness and the purpose
and His master plan.
I pray that all will travel His way and become pure
in heart and find His righteousness so that
we all can take his hand.

Matthew 6:33
But seek ye first the kingdom of God, and His righteousness;

A Prayer As A Poem — Richard A. Dixon

February 7

May I Continue To Be Faithful

I pray on this day to be labeled by his word,
His Sharing, His Caring, and let
me give all I can give.
I pray only to be judged by the standard of the
spirit of my God in the fullness of
the life that I live.
I pray to God not to be rated by the world's
community and by my
materialistic gains.
It is my ultimate goal to do His will and
not to accumulate worldly
goods and fame.
I pray that we will see the handwriting on the wall
and open our hearts to each other
to do what we should.
It is only through the moral laws of His heaven
that we are guided and to receive all
of His spiritual goods.

Proverbs 15:6
In the house of the righteous is much treasure:———

A Prayer As A Poem — Richard A. Dixon

February 8

One Day We Will See And Know All

On this day I pray that I will not worry about
the things that are not quite clear
in my mind.
I pray they will become more vivid to me and because
of His spiritual help, eventually they will
be well-defined.
I pray that because of my continuous striving in getting closer to Him, my knowledge will increase
from day to day.
I pray that I will become wiser about things in
life and may that picture of life becomes
a beautiful portrait.
I pray that I will forever understand that my
trust and faith in Him will indeed take
away all of my fear.
I know that one day, without any doubts, all of the
things that I cannot see now will someday
become crystal clear.

Psalm 37:5
Commit thy way unto the LORD; trust————And he shall bring it to pass.
A Prayer As A Poem—Richard A. Dixon

February 9

To Commune With Him

Let me pray on this day that I will qualify this moment
to take time out to commune with my God
with my very soul.
I pray to remain smart on the fact that if I only
use my head, the virtues of
heaven may never unfold.
In all of my prayers I must remember at all times
to shut down my physical senses to com-
municate with my savior.
For it is only through the life-line of the spirit that
I can get a glimpse of the wonders of the heavens
in its entire splendor.
I pray that I will continue to pray earnestly
and for each day this is how I will hope
that each will begin.
I pray by my spiritual loving efforts I will be
able to commune with my LORD
forever amen.

Revelation 3:20
Behold I stand at the door and knocking; if any man hear
my voice, and open the door, I will come in———

A Prayer As A Poem — Richard A. Dixon

February 10

My Troubleshooter Will Take Care Of It

On this day I pray that I will not be
controlled by any problem that
comes my way.
I pray to quickly put it all in His hands,
so my mind will not be taunted
and go astray.
For it is known that when I try to take care
of the situation and do what I think
should be done,
The situation gets thrown out of proportion,
what started out as a ounce of trouble,
turns into a megaton.
I pray that my attitude toward life has
changed to the point that I know that
God will see me through.
I know and pray that He will not allow any-
thing to destroy my soul as long as
my heart is open and true.

Psalm 27:5
For in the time of trouble He shall hide me in His pavilion———

A Prayer As A Poem — Richard A. Dixon

February 11

Putting Patience In Your Life

Let me pray on this day that I will be cognizance
that patience for each other
should be secured.
I pray that each and everyone should put
forward an effort so spiritual life
can be assured.
We all know that we must come to the reality that
none of us are without some sort of wrong that
plagues us along the way.
We must all pray that with understanding that a
positive resolve can be obtained not
for tomorrow but for today.
I pray that our true love for each other will
continue to bring that total agreement
and harmony for all.
I pray that with our frailties our relations can
still be positive and lasting by using
that patience protocol.

2 Peter 1:6
And to knowledge temperance; and to temperance patience———

A Prayer As A Poem—Richard A. Dixon

February 12

Getting Rid Of Our Negative

On this day I pray that I will concentrate and to
know that I cannot stop praying to rid myself
of my negative self.
Let me continue to strive to eliminate that self
within me so there will be no more
of that negative left.
For I know that it is only that self that lets us
know whenever hurt is viewed and it comes
to us with a damaging blast.
I pray that I will reach that point in life when
hurt to me will just be a earthly
thing of the past.
I pray to take myself out of the forefront
and have compassion for those
who hurt me.
I pray to find all of the loving answers that will
resolve these situations and set all of
our hearts free.

Proverbs 18:19
A brother offended is harder to be won than a strong city———

A Prayer As A Poem — Richard A. Dixon

February 13

Live Now And Let God Govern Your Future

On this day, this twenty-four hours, I pray and
give thanks for the blessings that
I will receive today.
One day at a time, knowing what's in the future
could bring terror to our minds and
cause much disarray.
Basically, we should daily start by praying and
surrender to Him our will and
do His will.
It is known by now that He knows what's best
and He will sort out for us
what is real.
I pray that I will not hassle myself and be
comfortable with what the
future may bring.
I pray that I will primarily concern myself with
the presence and find peace the spirituality
of everything.

2 Corinthians 6:2
(For he saith)———BEHOLD, NOW IS THE ACCEPTED TIME; BEHOLD, NOW IS THE DAY OF SALVATION.

A Prayer As A Poem — Richard A. Dixon

February 14

Valentine's Day Done God's Way

On this day I pray that we will spiritually seek
and find the meaning of what is
Valentine's Day.
Let that search be so divine that we can vision
Cupid and his arrow traveling
God's pathway.
Honest true love should and can be spotlighted
to show others just how wonderful and
happy life can be.
Doing special things directly from the heart, assimi-
lating what is done in heaven, depicting some
of God's chivalry
Experiencing heaven on earth, hearts joining
together as one, feeling like angels, being
glorified in every way.
I pray that we find those significant reasons so that
all of those earthly exploitations will not be a part
of your Valentine's Day.

Luke 10:21
And He answered saying, "Thou shall love the LORD thy with all thou heart, and with all thou soul———And thou neighbor as thyself".

A Prayer As A Poem — Richard A. Dixon

February 15

The Word Is Righteous

Let me pray on this day to diligently find those
inner thoughts to guide me daily on
the right path.
I pray that negatives will not enter my mind so
that I will receive the rewards of
a positive aftermath.
I pray to continuously exercise this spiritual
action of good In order to maintain
that spiritual accord.
For it is through this righteousness that I
can be utilized as a channel for the
word of the LORD.
I know I must be faithful and discipline myself to
obtain that righteousness and strength that
I need to carry on.
I pray with the help of the power of my LORD
I will forever be in the spirit
from dawn to dawn.

1 Timothy 6:11
But thou O man of God, flee these Things, and follow after righteousness———

A Prayer As A Poem — Richard A. Dixon

February 16

Not Just Thankful But Humbly Thankful

On this day I pray that I will never be remiss
in being thankful for all that my
God has given me.
I know that He has given me more than I ever deserve and I know He will give more than
I can ever foresee.
To my forgiving LORD, I humbly thank Him for
all the blessings and the worldly gifts to
enhance my life.
Yes, it is my forgiving LORD and it is only through
His grace that I can live spiritually
without sinful strife.
I pray that through knowing these things and receiving the knowledge that my Almighty is the
reason for all that is good.
I pray in continuing being thankful that He will
continue to bless and guide me as He has done
since my early childhood.

Ephesians 5:20
Giving thanks always for all things Unto the God the Father and in the name of our Lord Jesus Christ.

A Prayer As A Poem — Richard A. Dixon

February 17

Love For All

Let me pray on this day that my heart will
forever overflow with love for
all mankind.
With this understanding that we are children
of God and His wish is no one to
be left behind.
I pray that my love will be transformed into
a spiritual tool to lend help and
hope for others.
For it is known that God is our heavenly
father so that makes us all as
sisters and brothers.
I pray on this day that I will do my part to
strengthen that bond between each and
every one of us.
I pray to continue to pass on my love to others,
to succeed to come together by keeping
the faith and trust.

John 15:17
These things I command you, That you love one another———

A Prayer As A Poem — Richard A. Dixon

February 18

A Call To All Sinners

On this day I pray for all of those souls who are
so deep in torment and fear and live
constantly in the dark.
I pray that they will somehow listen for the voices
that are in their souls and nurture that God
giving divine spark.
For the Almighty alone with your will power can
change that hate to love and fill your soul with
faith, hope, and joy.
I pray for those to know that their eternal life is voided
and they should become pure in heart, these virtues
they should employ.
I pray that all will actively turn their divine
spark into a flame to light the world and the
heavens so all will see.
I pray that we all will cease that life that characterize a sinner and will become a winner in
being a spiritual marquee.

Matthew 9:13
———I WILL HAVE MERCY, AND NOT
SACRIFICE: For I came not to call the righteous,
but sinners to repentance.

A Prayer As A Poem—Richard A. Dixon

February 19

My Everlasting Friend

I pray on this day and everyday to give thanks
to my Almighty for His everlasting
spiritual connection.
I pray and thank Him for He has come to me and
maintains that link as a friend and given
me positive direction.
I know that this glorious relationship has been
made possible and transformed my life
to a life to do good.
I recognize that without His guidance, my chances
of being where I am today would probably
not be a likelihood.
I pray that all will someday make Him their friend,
for joy and peace will be the things that
they will receive the most.
Getting that power and strength from Him, as a
friend, cannot be equaled and I am here to
shout it and to boast.

John 15:13
There is no greater love of man than this, that a man lay down his life for a friend.

A Prayer As A Poem — Richard A. Dixon

February 20

Abide In Him

On this day I pray that I will devote my
full attention to abide in Him
at anytime.
I pray that none of the bad things of the world
will interfere with me with their
negative slim.
My heart is open to Him and it tells me in
abiding in Him that He will be
there when I call.
I must be ready by blocking the world out, to
hear His voice and to allow my soul
to hear it all.
I pray today that my every moment will be
available to hear His words to guide
me along the way.
For when I discern that He is always in my
presence, I know all of my time was
quality time spent today.

John 15:4
Abide in me and I in you. As the branch Cannot bear fruit of itself———

A Prayer As A Poem — Richard A. Dixon

February 21

Being Able To Do It His Way

On this day I pray that I will be able to do every-
thing God's way and that I will
be totally discrete.
I pray that I will stand tall against all that
is wrong and bring good to
all that I meet.
To those that are weak, I pray that I can show
them where they can find that strength
to carry on.
I pray that I will have that spiritual capacity to
assist those in the dark and show them the light
of the dawn.
From this day forward, I pray that I will always be
a channel for the LORD to help others to
be spiritually steady.
I pray, whatever might happen in this oscillating
world, we can face it all and together we will
be spiritually ready.

Revelation 6:17
When the great day of His wrath comes; And who shall
be able to stand.

A Prayer As A Poem — Richard A. Dixon

February 22

Finding That Power That Comes From Above

I pray on this day not to succumb to the world
and surrender to those things that
will make me weary.
I believe I cannot do God's work right and I will
be of little help to myself and others
being tired and dreary.
I pray that I will turn away from the world and
quickly look for the genuine things of the spirit on
which the soul survives.
I pray to be strengthened by the powers of the
heavens, for then I can indeed help others
to improve their lives.
I pray then to be able to remove the weariness
out of the world and give hope and character
to all I see and meet.
I pray that I can move that spiritual energy
to help others to find God and make their
lives spiritually complete.

Isaiah 40:31
But they that wait upon the LORD shall renew their strength;————they shall run and not be weary————

A Prayer As A Poem — Richard A. Dixon

February 23

You Can't Sit On The Fence And Grow

Let me pray on this day that I will not be the
one that sits on the fence trying to decide
which way to go.
I pray that I will be decisive in my doing of
what is right, for my purpose is
to spiritually grow.
On this day I will not put first the things that
will give me the recognition in the form
of worldly gains.
I pray that I will concentrate on the doings of
being guided by God and to these ends,
I will maintain.
On this day I will live it as though it was
my last and I will give to it all of
my heart and soul.
I know by developing with His word is the way,
so I must not stop, I must continue
my spiritual role.

Ephesians 6:7
With good will doing service, as to the LORD, and not to men.

A Prayer As A Poem — Richard A. Dixon

February 24

Let Your Light Shine

Let me pray on this day and acknowledge that God
gave us the power to think and to do
what is right,
and He gave us that divine spark and if we ignore
and forget that, it will allow the world to lead us
away from the light.
To all of those who seems helplessly lost, I pray
they will dig deep down inside of
themselves and reach.
I pray that they will reach and nurture that spark
and remember how the word of the
LORD is preached.
Let us turn that divine spark into a flame that
will help light the kingdom of heaven
in all hearts.
Let us Pray for that divine torch and let our light
shine on His path and show all others exactly
where to start.

Matthew 5:16
Let your light so shine before men, that they may see your good works and glorify your Father.

A Prayer As A Poem — Richard A. Dixon

February 25

The Gifted Ones

On this day I pray to welcome all of our
fellowman attributes and their
spiritual gifted way.
Because of our forgiving Almighty, these gifts are
given to them as they are given to me, to actively
put on display.
It is a privilege to be given and possess the holy
spirit so that we can pass it on in the
name of grace.
I pray that we will use them at all times
especially when opportunity
shows its face.
I pray that whenever we are in the spiritual zone,
working with His gifts, to know
it's from above.
We must persevere because you just might be that
channel used by God to influence others to pass
on His love.

John 6:23
For the wages of sin is death; but the gift of God is eternal
life through Jesus Christ———

A Prayer As A Poem—Richard A. Dixon

February 26

Be Still And Be Tolerant

I pray on this day that I will be positive
and utilize the behavior
of tolerance.
Let me fully understand that life with
others is indeed a principal
to advance.
I pray that we all are in agreement that by
being still at times could be the prudent
thing to do.
With this foresight, we could turn what
could have been a bad situation into a
positive breakthrough.
I pray that we will all remember that our
Almighty is the most tolerant
of us all.
In spite of all the negative things that we do,
He will never hesitate to come to us
whenever we call.

Psalm 103:8
The LORD is merciful and gracious. slow to anger, and plentiful in mercy-

A Prayer As A Poem — Richard A. Dixon

February 27

Feeling That Strength From Within

On this day I pray that I will treasure my quiet
times, meditations, and communions that
I spend with Him.
When I am in these moments, I can feel all of
that spiritual strength building and
increasing from within.
When I am in prayer with Him there is a surge
of energy that rushes through
my very soul.
When I am in this glorious zone, it immediately
tells me the meaning of life and what
are my real goals.
I give credit to God and His capacity to transform
that glorious strength to do good, for it is due
to His amazing grace.
I pray that now we will all pray to Him so that we
will be blessed and His ordained strength will be
ours to forever embrace.

2 Samuel 22:33
God is my strength and power: And He makes my way perfect-

A Prayer As A Poem — Richard A. Dixon

February 28

Know The Meaning Of Love

On this day I pray to see that love is not only a
word within itself that signifies
positive power.
You should know that love has that spiritual way
of changing you from a spine to a
beautiful flower.
Know that you are blessed when the love that
you give to God above shows him
that you care.
Without any delay, He will continue to give you grace
and will give you His heaven for He wishes you
to be the heir.
One of His prime objectives in God's will is in loving
all people, especially when we reach out and
give others help.
There is one more prime thought to succeed and that
is to remember the Cardinal rule, do not forget
to love yourself.

Ephesians 3:13
To know the love of Christ will give you Knowledge, that
you might be filled with the fullness———

A Prayer As A Poem — Richard A. Dixon

February 29

Leap Year Day—Leap day—Leap Year Day
Find Your Connection With This Day

I pray on this day that I will find some posi-
tive connection with this added day to
balance our months and time.
I pray to find that additional plus to make
me a better person to stay in tune
with GOD'S spiritual chimes.
It is that positive person that takes advantage of
that God giving extra time, to improve their
character and their lives.
It is sometimes prudent when you are given
an inch and you take that mile, this
is an opening to thrive.
I pray to do everything that my Lord Savior
Jesus Christ will do today for that
will be my ultimate choice.
I pray today that some how this will be a holy
incentive and that I will be Spiritually
attentive in listening for His voice.

2 Peter 3:8
But beloved, be not ignorant of this one thing, that one day with the LORD is as a thousand———

A Prayer As A Poem—Richard A. Dixon

March 1

How Wonderful It Is To Be Blessed

I pray on this day and I am thankful that my
Almighty got a hold of my hand and I am
indeed daily blessed.
I thank my God that I got up this morning filled
with the spirit and like the rest of His flock, I
am not depressed.
I can remember that somewhere along the way
my life was once in the dark and I did not
know which way to go.
I made and took an earnest effort and came to
Him in earnest prayer and He glorified my
life and made it glow.
I pray that somehow we all can walk together
on His lighted path as spiritual
sisters and brothers.
Now I pray that His light that shines on
me will become a glorious
beam for others.

Numbers 6:24-25
The LORD bless thee and keep thee:
The LORD make his face shine upon thee———

A Prayer As A Poem—Richard A. Dixon

March 2

Expect Only Good Things For Yourself

On this day I pray that I will maintain
that faith that good will follow
me through this day.
I pray to continue that consistency of mind
and be positive and believe
better will come my way.
I would like it to be known that because of my
faith, my vision of life is to stay faithful
for I am a believer.
I pray that in my quest that all of my
fellowmen will join me and become
spiritual achievers.
It is a known fact that you can face the world better
by developing spiritually and receiving His
gifts by doing His will.
As a believer who comes to the Almighty in
prayer, He will assure each day that your
hearts will be refilled.

Psalm 23:6
Surely goodness and mercy shall follow me all the days of my life: and I shall dwell in the house of the LORD———

A Prayer As A Poem — Richard A. Dixon

March 3

No One Needs Slanderous Gossip

I pray on this day that I will not be guilty
of any negative words about
those around me.
I pray that my words will be positive and
constructive and the answer
to eliminate misery.
I pray that I will understand that we are here
by the grace of God and we should
show that bonding.
It is that ill-thinking alone that can divide our
spiritual house as love always should be our
source of responding.
It is on the wings of our sharing and caring for
each other that will complete our spiritual
goals in all of our lives.
I pray that I will never forget to stay positive and
to be helpful to others for this is the will of God
for our way to survive.

Corinthians 13:6
Rejoice not in iniquity, but rejoice in the truth———

A Prayer As A Poem — Richard A. Dixon

March 4

Accept His Guidance

I pray on this day that I will accept and do
everything that is guided
by my LORD.
I pray that even the little things that I do will bring
my heart and His heart
in one accord.
I know that at the end of the day according to
His decisions the conclusions will
be fine for me.
For leaving everything in His hands, the best
for me will come and give me
genuine serenity.
I pray and know that my Almighty understands every
thing about me and there are no secrets that
I can keep from Him.
I pray that my only choice will be to maintain my
honesty, love, and faith, and with my will power,
I will take this stand.
I pray that I will reside in the spiritual world and
relax for this day, for my guidance and day is
in my Almighty's hands.

Luke 1:79
To give light to them that sit in darkness and in the shadow
of death, to guide our feet into the way of truth———

A Prayer As A Poem—Richard A. Dixon

March 5

Just Do Good

On this day I pray that I will not use
any excuses for doing something
that is wrong.
I pray to keep walking on that path that leads
to goodness so that it will
keep me strong.
I know I cannot keep leaning on those things
and say that justice in this world is
not my friend.
I pray to build my character in looking to my
God and those spiritual forces that He
develops from within.
I cannot preoccupy my life too much with only those
so-called treasures that I acquire
from the earth.
For they will bring me temporary pleasures and the
misery at the end is really only what they
are really worth.
I pray I will concentrate on what my Almighty
can give me to keep me from the
darkness of sin.
By doing it His way, I need no excuse for doing
evil, for my world of good will be
spiritually built-in.

Romans 12:21
Be not overcome of evil, but overcome evil with
good———

A Prayer As A Poem — Richard A. Dixon

March 6

Acknowledge Him

On this day I pray I will acknowledge that
it is only through His grace that
I am blessed.
I know that what my LORD has given me is
considerably more, although my efforts are
considerably less.
For some of us, it is not mindful that it is God's
plan to give us a chance to
come to Him.
For if it was only left to our decision to get
into heaven, our chances would be
close to slim.
Striving to be perfect and sinless are goals
that we will probably never be
able to achieve.
I pray that in that positive striving it will mean
the most in keeping the faith and
continuing to believe.

Proverbs 3:6
In all thy way acknowledge Him, and He shall
direct———

A Prayer As A Poem — Richard A. Dixon

March 7

The Working Spirit

I pray on this day that I will be a soul that
is targeted by a surge of
His spiritual flow.
Let the world know that I am with the Almighty and
that is why I am a friend of the world and blessing
for my foe.
I pray that I will help spread that glorious
spirit to all today to show them
that God is good.
May that spirit enter all of their souls and that
stream continues until His
knowledge is understood.
I pray because of all of our efforts that this
spiritual force will make a ripple through
the heavenly sky.
I pray that it will become known for all
to see that we will be believers until
the day we die.

Isaiah 11:2
And the spirit of the LORD shall rest upon him, The spirit of wisdom and understanding, ———The spirit of knowledge and of the fear of the LORD———

A Prayer As A Poem — Richard A. Dixon

March 8

A Channel For My God Once More

I pray on this day that I may again be given the
opportunity to become a channel to do what
my God will have me to do.
May I do my best in my spiritual efforts and take
this sacred privilege to render
good in all that I ensue.
When I have that control, my will power to
accept the will of my Almighty is a fact
of being blessed.
The glorious thought alone is a miracle to know
that God has selected me to be a link to form
this heavenly crest.
For in doing the work of the LORD is that gift
of grace that is given to those that come
to Him again and again.
With this spiritual connection that has been
made, I pray to be a channel
to rid all that is sin.

Romans 8:28
And we know that all things work together for good to them that love God, to them who are called according———

A Prayer As A Poem—Richard A. Dixon

March 9

Redeeming Our Lives

On this day I pray for all of us who were once
completely lost in the darkness of sin,
stress, and torment.
I thank God for redeeming us and giving us grace
to nurture our divine spark to make sure our
lives are well-spent.
It is understood that by coming to Him it is
the only way to find the inner peace that
our Almighty can give.
By putting everything in His hands, our hands
became free to grasp His spirit so
that we may live.
We know that because of Christ on the cross at
Calvary as believers, we are forgiven
for our many transgressions.
We know that on the day that we came to Him,
by the grace of our LORD, we were reborn
when we made our confessions.

Psalm 107:2
Let the redeemed of the LORD say so, whom He has redeemed From the hand of the enemy———

A Prayer As A Poem — Richard A. Dixon

March 10

Showing Gratitude At All Times

On this day I pray that I will place attention
and show my gratitude to my God
for all of my blessings.
For I am humbly thankful for being brought
out of the pit of darkness and
all of its depressions.
Sometimes because of my frailties, I have found
myself not showing my thanks for the good
fortune that came my way.
I pray and I know that my Almighty is
always by my side even though
my mind does go astray.
From this day on, I pray always that I will
have a thankful heart for all of the things
that God has done for me.
I pray that I will always count my blessings,
for every right thing comes from God and
that is a spiritual guarantee.

Ephesians 5:20
Giving thanks always for all things unto God———and in the name of our Lord Jesus Christ.

A Prayer As A Poem — Richard A. Dixon

March 11

Entering The Kingdom Of God

I pray on this day that I will continue to understand exactly what I can take with me into
the hereafter or the beyond
I know that the worldly gains will not be an accepted standard, for it might be harder for the
rich to enter than the vagabond.
I believe that it is only those things that are given
up by the spiritual soul that can travel
to that heavenly sphere.
To make that trip to God's kingdom, we will
have to have a loving honest heart
that makes us sincere.
Love, unselfishness, purity, truthfulness, I pray
to have these things of the spirit that
last forevermore.
Helping others, caring and sharing for each other
are the criterions to enter and pass through
His Kingdom Door.

Matthew 16:26
For what is a man profited, if he gain The whole world, and lose his soul———

A Prayer As A Poem — Richard A. Dixon

March 12

Evil Will Not Have Dominion Over Me

I pray on this day that I will not allow
anything to take dominion over my
God given serenity.
I pray that my inner peace will be protected by the forces of my
God the Almighty.
I pray that my God will give me the power
to protect me from the
world of torment.
I pray that He will give me that strength to
shield me from all evil and its
negative intents.
I pray that others will see that they can also find
that glorious security by taking refuse
in His spiritual word.
Pray to Him and rid yourself of worry, for His
dominion will assure your peace
will not be disturbed.

Romans 6:14
For sin shall not have dominion over you: For you are not under the law but under grace.

A Prayer As A Poem — Richard A. Dixon

March 13

As A Christian

I pray on this day that I will fully understand
all of the spiritual blessings of being
a believer of Christianity.
I pray to be at peace for it is a blessing to
know that our sins were forgiven because
of the cross on Calvary.
Some of us believe that we will receive grace
according to our efforts in doing what
we think is right.
As Christians, we know that we are given more
grace than we deserve for our God wants
us all to unite.
I pray that one day we will all see the answer
and find out that our spirituality is not based
on a human force.
We will find that it is through our forgiving
LORD that we are blessed and He is
our only spiritual source.

1 Peter 4:16
Yet if any man suffer as a Christian, let him not be ashamed; but let him glorify God on this behalf———

A Prayer As A Poem — Richard A. Dixon

March 14

Only His Words From My Heart

On this day I pray that the only words that come
from my head will be compassionate
in being positive.
I pray that my heart will take control and I
pray that the spirit in my conscious will
be more than active.
For it is far too many times that the wrong
words are said when emotions
take over our minds.
Most of us know that it only takes a split second
to let that negative in to get us off
our spiritual guidelines.
I pray in living the way that the Almighty will
have me to live and making His thoughts
my thoughts at all times.
I pray today to strive for that perfection so
that my actions transform in being His
will and none will be mine.

Colossians 3:16
Let the word of Christ dwell in you richly In all wisdom———

A prayer As a Poem — Richard A. Dixon

March 15

Getting That Daily Supply Of Spiritual Needs

I pray on this day that I will be strengthened
when that flow of God's spirit to
me is transmitted.
I pray and know in having His power, I will
be successful and my heart will be
completely committed.
I pray that I will set aside that quality time
and be available for Him to
give me His gift.
I pray and know I will be amongst the blessed
in receiving his grace that will give
me a spiritual lift.
I pray that my fellowman will understand, to
really live, our hearts need that daily
energy from above.
I pray that all of us will get down on our knees
daily and pray and ask the LORD for this
daily supply of love.

Philippians 4:19
But my God shall supply all your need According to his riches in glory by Jesus Christ———

A Prayer As A Poem — Richard A. Dixon

March 16

A Time To Rest

On this day I pray that I will know when
to stop my action and allow
myself to rest.
I pray that I will understand that I must not
ever overwork for I may
not do my best.
It is good in my period of rest that I make direct
contact with my LORD and I should ask
Him for guidance.
It is at these times I pray to Him and I prepare
my day and he guides me away
from evil stridence.
I pray that I will always recognize the fact that I
need religious action and rest in
my daily plan.
By resting with my Almighty, He will give me
that daily strength to do well as a
spiritual workingman.
It is only through proper planning that you
know when to extend yourself in efforts
and when to be still.
I pray that I will know that difference and
perform His work successfully
as He so wills.

Psalm 37:7
Rest in the LORD and wait patiently for fret Not
thyself———

A Prayer As A Poem — Richard A. Dixon

March 17

Let Them Be Tears From Heaven

I pray on this day for everyone who may be
experiencing hurt and their tears
are tears of pain.
I pray that their hearts and souls will become
opened and that they become a part
of God's holy chain.
We all cry at times, either because of a physical
hurt or something or someone has
hurt us deep inside.
Life sometimes does not seems fair to us, but
we should put it in God's hand, for in
Him we should confide.
I pray that we will come to our senses and realize that our selfishness causes much that
puts us in torment.
If we take ourselves out of the spotlight, we will
find a spiritual cure to take care of
many of those ailments.
The most wonderful time of your life would
be when you put God in your life to free
you from anxiety and fears.
Praying will indeed make you feel better inside and
when you cry, you will cry with joy for God
will be in your tears.

2 Timothy 1:4
Greatly desiring to see thee, being mindful Of their tears, that I may have that feel of joy———

A Prayer As A Poem — Richard A. Dixon

March 18

In Death We Eternally Live

I pray on this day that I will be free of
fear because of what death
may bring.
I pray that I can see that ultimate reason for
the resurrection Of Christ that makes our
hearts sing.
As believers, we all know that in God's promise
we will experience a resurrection and be
raised from the dead.
It is all because of our Almighty's master plan
for Christ on the cross died for our sins
to make us unafraid.
I pray that we will all see that death is not as
final as it is conceived by those who
are not believers.
I pray that we will understand that we will find
life after dying and our God will make us
the eternal receivers.
In all of our minds, let our hearts be completely aware of this manifestation that
only God can give.
Let us all keep the faith and rejoice in His spirit
to know that it is in death that
we eternally live.

John 5:24
Verily, verily, I say unto you, he that heareth my word, and beliveth on him that sent me, hath everlasting life———

A Prayer As A Poem — Richard A. Dixon

March 19

Commit To His Way

On this day I pray not to interfere in
any way with any of
God's work.
I pray that I will understand my
part in finding the things that
we search.
In these times my duties will be to pray
and to do things positive to help
make things right.
Keeping love and compassion in my plans
as being a channel to perform
my spiritual fight.
I pray that I will respond in the Almighty's
way for he will help me improve
my spiritual skills.
By leaving everything to Him for now, the future
will be better and life as we live it will be
closer to real.

Psalm 37:5
Commit thy way unto the LORD; trust also In Him; and he shall bring it to pass———

A Prayer As A Poem — Richard A. Dixon

March 20

Thanks For A New Day To Do Good

I pray on this day and give thanks for a
chance to start a new day and to
be pro-life.
In my negatives that I did wrong in the past, I ask
for forgiveness and I pray today will be
without strife.
I pray and believe that my LORD will forgive those
who are honest and have the purest of intentions
in living His way.
I pray that I will forever strive to put to rest all of
those frailties of the past and I will be
at my best today.
On this day I pray that I have been given more
grace and a new beginning
to get it right.
I pray that any negatives will not bother me and I
will continue to bond with others so
that we all unite.

Ephesians 5:20
Giving thanks always to the Father in the name of our Lord Jesus Christ———

A Prayer As A Poem—Richard A. Dixon

March 21

Praying In Secret But Rewarded Openly

On this day I pray to know that it is not so
important that I pray aloud so that
others may hear.
By following this pattern of praying I may be
distracted at times and my meaning may
not be clear.
I pray that I will understand that I will need to
set aside a quiet time away from the
noise of the land.
I will need to find a secluded place to reach out
to my LORD and empty my heart and put
it all in His hands.
By knowing all of these things, I pray in secret
today with a joy in my heart that is pure
and that sings.
I pray and know that he will reward me openly so
others can see His glow and that He is indeed the
King of Kings.

Matthew 6:6
But when you pray enter the closet, and when you have shut then door, pray to the Father which is in secret; ——
——reward openly————

A Prayer As A Poem — Richard A. Dixon

March 22

Vengeance Is His – Not Ours

I pray on this day that I will not face this world
and declare myself god in being judgmental of
my sisters and brothers.
I pray that I will not hold onto the negative issues
that will only agitate me, but
also many, many others.
I pray that I will not be pushed into a
situation that will cause some
violence after effect.
The question should be answered on why am I
taking the role that should be resolved
by God's architect.
None of us should use revenge as an active retaliation, to put it in His hands would be the
right way to respond.
This is not a sign of weakness, this indicates that
you put your faith and trust in God to resolve
a positive bond.
I pray that I will always know that patience
and spiritual understanding
will be my only guidelines.
For I will leave His work for Him for He
alone can judge, for the LORD said,
"VENGEANCE WILL BE MINE".

Deuteronomy 32:35
To me belongeth vengeance, and recompence; Their foot shall slide in due time———

A Prayer As A Poem — Richard A. Dixon

A Prayer As A Poem For Each Day

March 23

Never Stop Praying For Others

I pray on this day that all will take a few minutes
and form some quality time to
pray for others.
The blessings that come from these positive efforts
could make the difference of a
life of another.
I pray that we will notice that it is in the lack of our
praying for each other that we
suffer at times.
God only knows just what the number is on how
many resolves came together because of
our Praying line.
The power of prayer, to most, I believe is not
taken seriously as a spiritual tool to
get things done.
I pray that the believers can somehow show
them that it is because of prayer, daily
battles are consistently won.
O God, I pray that I will do my part in getting
down on my knees this day to
pray for my fellowman.
I know that my LORD is always listening to all
of those honest hearts who want all to
reach His promised land.

James 5:16
Confess your faults one to another, And pray one for another that you may the effectual fervent prayer of a righteous man———

A Prayer As A Poem — Richard A. Dixon

March 24

From The Dark To The Light

On this day I pray for all that have not found
that path that leads them out of the dark
into the light.
I pray that they will kindle their divine spark so
that the heavenly beam will come
into their sights.
Sometimes our spirits are so low and we lose
our way and we cannot find hope in
anything that we do.
I pray that we will all trust and believe that the
Almighty will always give us that strength
to see us through.
Your life is in discord, God will bring you order,
He will get rid of your turmoil and give
you peace and rest.
I pray that all will find that power by coming to the
LORD Almighty so He can make your
life a glorious success.
I pray that I will forever be humbly thankful for
all of His grace and that I will eternally
live His will and His way.
I pray that I will never allow the world to distract
me in my goings for I know I receive His
grace whenever I pray.

Act 26:18
To open their eyes, and to turn them from darkness to light, and from the power of Satan unto God———

A Prayer As A Poem — Richard A. Dixon

March 25

Be Guided By The Spirit Not Frustrations

I pray on this day that my coming and going
will not be interfered with by any
degree of frustration.
I pray that my mind will be guided by the spirit
of my LORD and will not fall into
confusing stagnation.
It is at these times that we are in a state of
confusion and its torment leaves us
with little or no defense.
I pray that I will find the answers in my communion with my LORD and I will use
his guidance as my offense.
I pray from this day on that I will find the
strength to fight this mind problem that
puts my life in a decline.
I pray that through my prayers and listening to
His words that I can rid myself of
this frustration for all times.

2Timothy 1:7
For God has not given us the spirit of fear; but of power
of love, and of sound mind———

A Prayer As A Poem — Richard A. Dixon

March 26

Think - Say - And Do (TSD)

On this day I pray that I will think, say, and
do God's will with all my
heart and soul.
Thinking, saying, and doing good are those
collective traits that will keep you in
being spiritually whole.
I pray that I will keep my TSD's
all together in one
spiritual accord.
For one without the other in cooperating in
His spirit there will be
apparent discord.
I know that we cannot find truth in our character
if the goodness is not passed on in what we think
and what we say and do.
If there is no honesty, no consistent connection in
our TSD's, there will be trouble
in all that we ever pursue.
I pray that love will spiritually flow consistently
through these bonding connections and
will be guided by my LORD.
I will know then that I will have that assurance
that everything will be all right and this
will be my glorious reward.

Proverbs 23:7
For as he think in his heart, so is he———

A Prayer As A Poem — Richard A. Dixon

March 27

Not My Will But God's Will

I pray on this day that I will not stand in
the way of my LORD's master
plan for me.
There will be times that what I want to
happen in my life will bring
future misery.
I pray that my selfish self will be not found
to counteract the good that
comes my way.
I pray that my will is guided only by His spirit
so that my growth will have no blocks
and no delay.
Sometimes your search for happiness will point
you in a direction and tells
you to go west.
Your conscious or His spiritual presence will tell
you the difference, you should stop for
He knows what's best.
So I think hard and clear each time that I pray
that my heart and soul will commune
with Him one on one,
and that my heart and soul will be completely
in tune, knowing that it is not my will
but His will be done.

Matthew 6:10
Thy kingdom come. Thy will be done in Earth, as it is in heaven.

A Prayer As A Poem—Richard A. Dixon

March 28

Give To Others What You Have Received

I pray on this day that I have found that good-
ness within me to give away what
I have received.
I pray and thank my God for all of His spiritual
blessings because I have truly
come to believe.
It was indeed through my suffering, trials and
tribulations, my experience has
made me who I am.
My positive responses to my past problems and
failures has brought me peace and got rid
of that life of sham.
I pray now that I will give away all that I have
received so that others may be led
out of the dark.
I pray that my efforts will help others to look
deep into their soul and nurture that
God-given divine spark.
I pray that I will always understand that it is
only through my God that I can
continue to proceed.
I pray to see that by working with others and
working with Him is the only way that we
can spiritually succeed.

Matthew 5:42
Give to all that ask you to give and also do not deny those who wish to———

A Prayer As A Poem — Richard A. Dixon

March 29

Be A Winner And Worship Him

On this day I pray that I will receive all of the
divine blessings through worshiping Him that
will be freely given to me.
Now, I am totally aware that if I make my heart
available to Him always, His divine spirit
will be mine for eternity.
Your most inner spirit will encounter a posi-
tive revolutionary change that comes
from heaven alone.
By directing your honest thoughts toward the
heavens, His divine strength will make
you forever strong.
I pray that my consciousness of God will forever
be instilling in my mind for he is without a doubt
our Almighty king.
We should see that difference, that this world is an
earthly form that is only a temporary place for
His divine spiritual things.
I pray that through all of this understanding
that our lives and life will be raised to the
height of peace and serenity.
I pray that our earthly ways and human ways of
living will flow with the spirit into the sphere
of His glorious Divinity.

John 4:24
God is the spirit and when we worship Him, we should
worship Him in spirit And truth.———

A Prayer As A Poem — Richard A. Dixon

March 30

He Restores My Life

On this day I pray and give thanks to my God
for restoring my spirit and giving me
a new way to live.
I have been liberated from those things of the
earth that have blocked the flow of
good that He gives.
Through my new life, I have given up many
things that I once desired and thought they
were right for me.
Since I have eliminated them from my life, I
can now feel His spirit and His happiness
in every single degree.
I pray that all will open their hearts and let
the spirit flow within them.
He can give all of us all of His goodness of heaven
if only we come to Him.
He can and will restore all that come, His way is
pure in heart, for He can heal all
souls for eternity.
Now I pray that all will understand and give
thanks to Him for restoring us and making
our hearts free.

Psalm 23:3
He has restored my soul and He leads me to the path of righteousness———

A Prayer As A Poem — Richard A. Dixon

March 31

Be In Unity With His Laws

On this day I pray that I will be in unity with
all of the laws that God has handed
down to us.
I know that it is only by doing all of His will
that I can receive all of
His spiritual plus.
I pray that all of our brothers and sisters will know
that we must follow His moral laws as
best as we can.
If not, our spirit is broken or weakened to that proportion of what we do not do according to His law,
His master plan.
We certainly know if we do not follow the laws of
nature, our bodies will succumb to
some kind of misery.
I pray that we will see or get the picture that by
not following the moral laws we will
suffer spiritually.
I pray that we all face the facts that we cannot
fight the laws and there is no news that they
will ever change.
It will be best that we build and strengthen our
spirits together by doing His will and all
that He proclaims.

Psalm 119:174
I have always longed for the salvation of the LORD, for
His law is my law and delight———

A Prayer As A Poem — Richard A. Dixon

April 1

We The People Of God

On this day let me pray that I will not fall short
in regarding myself as a believer
in the eyes of my God.
I pray that the self esteem that I have gotten
from my faith will be seen by others
as one of His lighting rods.
I know that I have been blessed and it started by
being created by God and made in
His image as a man.
By coming to Him, He has given me the goodness
of life and instead of doubting myself,
I now say, "Yes I can".
I pray that it will be embedded deep in my soul
that through Jesus Christ, my sins are forgiven
and eternal life is mine.
I pray that these assurances will continue to give
me that faith and trust and on me His heavenly
light will forever shine.

1 Samuel 12:22
The LORD will not forsake His people for His great name sake because it has pleased the LORD to make us His people———

A Prayer As A Poem—Richard A. Dixon

April 2

Forever Fight Evil With Good

I pray on this day that the strength of my spirit
will be able to counteract the wrongs that
may come my way.
I pray no matter how much sin and trouble may
be there to block my love, I will persist
never to go astray.
As we live in this world things have gotten many
times worse and much has become
a complete outcast.
I pray that I will recognize the seriousness of it
all and fight those evils and be in control
when all is past.
I pray that we can see the devil working his evil
continuously, trying to take us away from
all that is good.
I pray that we will double our efforts to rid
ourselves of Lucifer and forever do the
things that we should.
I pray that I will forever be prepared and
ready without any fear to stand tall with
my LORD by His side.
I pray and will know that I will have all of the
heavenly weapons and have my
God as my spiritual guide.

1 Timothy 6:12
Always fight with the good of faith to secure a hold on eternal life———

A Prayer As A Poem—Richard A. Dixon

April 3

He Wants Us All To Live In His House

I pray that we will understand that our Almighty
is not just our creator to go to and
ask for His blessings.
He also wants us to come to Him and make Him
your home for this is a part of
our spiritual testing.
I pray that we will acknowledge that he is our
Father and He wants us to come and live
with Him and not just part-time.
He expects when you have moved into His home
that this would be permanent so no family
member will be left behind.
I pray that we will stop looking at our God as
just the Almighty creator and fulfilling our
lives in a miraculous way.
God wants each and every one of us to bring our
hearts and souls to Him and dwell with Him
starting each God-given day.

John 14:12
In my Father's house there are many mansions; I will go and prepare a place for you———

A Prayer As A Poem — Richard A. Dixon

April 4

Easter Brings Us The Purpose Of THE CROSS

I pray on this day that I will keep in my heart
the purpose of my Jesus who died for us and
saved us from our sins.
The vision of the cross followed my Jesus' life
from His very birth and it is in our hearts
and is deeply built in.
I pray that we can see that it was His crucifixion
that gave us His holy grace to bring
us back into His fold.
Because our God at our creation made us in His
image and He wanted us in His kingdom
and to save our souls.
I pray that we will never make that mistake and
think it was only another Christian that
was on the cross at Calvary.
For the glorious plan by our Almighty was His
love and grace and gift to all of us
to give us life for eternity.

Hebrews 12:2
Looking unto Jesus the author and finisher of our faith; who for the joy was set before Him endured the cross————

John 3:17
For God sent not His son into the world to condemn the world; but that the world through Him might be saved———

A Prayer As A Poem — Richard A. Dixon

April 5

He Will Heal Us

Let me pray on this day to my God and believe that
He can heal my spirit and will
cure me if only I ask.
He sees all of the hidden torment and He knows
who we are, though at times
we hide behind a mask.
Unmistakably, God knows it all and He will
always come to us to heal us and to make
us holy, healthy and strong.
He could easily become our family
doctor even though He sits
on the highest throne.
I pray that we can confide in Him and
trust Him to take away all
of our spiritual pain.
I pray that we can see that He can make
us new and your spirit will
be joyfully ordained.
I pray that my fears will be cast to the side and
my heart and soul will be opened to
accept His full treatment.
To allow the healing of His spirit to flow within
me, everything then will be all right for
His work is heavenly sent.

Psalm 6:2
Have mercy on me, O LORD, for I am weak; O LORD
heal me———

A Prayer As A Poem — Richard A. Dixon

April 6

One God, One World, One Life

I pray on this day that I will forever be a
part of God's spiritual collective
world of good and love.
I walk on the face of this earth as an individual, I pray that we come together and
fit like a spiritual glove.
By His grace, the Almighty gave us the
power to think as one and to come to
make important decisions.
Through our experiences, we learn to make spiritual choices and my will is to put my life
under His supervision.
In this prayer we will find eternal life coming
together as one to give us power and
make us spiritually effective.
I pray that all will see their individual will power as a plus and thus help us to improve
and build His spiritual collective.

Ephesians 4:6
One God and Father of all, who is above all, and through all, and in you all———

A Prayer As A Poem — Richard A. Dixon

April 7

To Find That Heavenly Joy With God

On this day I pray that I will always travel that
road that leads to the land of joy
with my LORD.
I pray that I will maintain that level of love in my
heart that will assure me of enjoying
His spiritual awards.
It is known that it must be borne in the mind that
it is through service that we find
Christian satisfaction.
We become overjoyed with that happiness in
our hearts because we have shown pure love
with a godly action.
I pray that we all will see the positive and the
power that we can receive by yielding
kindness to our fellowman.
By going with the flow of our soul we become
a part of the purpose of life, we become
part of God's plan.
I pray that we will find that joy in doing service
for others and that our behavior is only apart
of our caring technique.
When we discover that by rendering good
deeds, we find that complete joy, and is it
not what we primarily seek?

Colossians 3:24
Knowing that of the LORD you shall receive the reward
———for ye serve the Lord Christ.

A Prayer As A Poem — Richard A. Dixon

April 8

The Right Decision Is God's Decision

I pray on this day that no matter how terrible a
disaster may come my way, my trust
in God remains strong.
I will always keep that faith knowing that His
decision for me is right although some
may think it was wrong.
I pray that I will understand that life in this
world will only last for a split second
compared to eternity.
It is written in my God's master plan to make our
address permanent in His kingdom
for you and me.
Pray and let there be no doubts when you compre-
hend that He sees what lies ahead for us, He can
save us from lots of pain.
When our loved ones are taken away from us, it
could be a sign of grace, a blessing in
disguise, our spiritual gain.

Psalm 19:8
The statutes of the LORD are right, by rejoicing the
heart, the commandment of the LORD is pure———

A Prayer As A Poem — Richard A. Dixon

April 9

Be And Do The Same As God

On this day I pray that my development in relat-
ing to all that the good in my life will
progress from glory to glory.
Let all believers come together to share their every
spiritual thought so we can continue
to build our spiritual story.
I pray that the laws of God will continue to prevail
so that we all will become more like
our LORD in every way.
I pray that we will all be so much alike that every
action will be alike and the words will be
all true in what we all say.
Living the life that our Almighty will have us to
live, walking and talking with Him
wherever we go.
In this life we will find similarities in all areas be-
coming more like our LORD, even our being
will begin to glow.
I pray that we all will come together to share our
glorious salvation process so that
all of us becomes one.
I pray that someday all of our hearts will beat
and feel the same so that our ultimate
battle can be won.

Romans 12:16
Be of the same mind one to another———

A Prayer As A Poem — Richard A. Dixon

April 10

I Pray That He Will Order My Steps

On this day I pray that I will not just sit and think
that my life will be free from the negatives
that life may bring.
Just because I am walking with Him does not mean
I will not have the usual problems as having
a cold in spring.
My spiritual ways of life will however be the key to
the fact that that my all-around living
would have gotten better.
I pray that I will always come up to the bat and
do my duties to perform and to maintain
my way as a pacesetter.
I pray that my Almighty will continue to order
my steps and that He will guide me and
I will never disagree.
I pray that He will bless and keep me when those
things go wrong and all that
might bring me Misery.
Finding that most inner peace and making
those prepared steps that came as
a gift from my LORD.
I pray and thank Him for being His walking
partner and making steps in cadence with
His in one accord.

Psalm 37:23
The steps of a good man are ordered by the LORD; and he delighteth in his way———

A Prayer As A Poem — Richard A. Dixon

April 11

We All Can Be Changed

I pray on this day for all to believe that every-
one can be changed by the spiritual
hand of the Creator.
By following our Almighty Father, he will make
our lives better and He will show us the
way as our navigator.
It is generally accepted that people deep-down
inside want to change from the
torments of their lives.
I pray that all of these people will becomes
believers so that their ways can be altered
and their spirit revived.
I pray that none of these people reside in the
notion that who they are now, is
now what you get.
Believing that God can make all things possible, he
can fill you heart with love
with no regrets.
I pray that each and every one of us will help
each other to change in the ways that God
will have us to change.
I pray that we will become more like our heavenly
Father so that our lives will be joyful
and spiritually arranged.

2 Corinthians 3:18
We all as in the glass of glory of the LORD are changed
into the same image from glory to glory———

A Prayer As A Poem — Richard A. Dixon

April 12

A Fortress And Thriving Roots

On this day I pray that my fortress of
spirit is steady and will be as
solid as a rock.
I pray that its foundation will be so embedded
that evil cannot disturb it no matter
how much it knocks.
I pray that all will understand that
my roots will be so deep
and so very strong.
I pray that all of my being will flourish and
grow and I will do positive
service all lifelong.
I pray to know that I must have those thriv
ing roots and a fortress that
can last to the end.
I pray that I will nourish my roots and constantly
reinforce my fortress to withstand
all evil and sin.

Psalm 31:3
For you are my rock and my fortress; therefore for thy name sake lead me and guide me———

A Prayer As A Poem — Richard A. Dixon

A Prayer As A Poem For Each Day

April 13

In The Counsel Of The LORD

On this day I pray not to depend on the
factions of hind-sight to find the
right things to do.
I pray that I will be given that spiritual in-
sight to resolve personal problems that
I presently pursue.
I pray that I will be smart and seek the
counsel of our LORD to show
me that right way.
I pray to be given that religious knowledge
so that a positive end can be
effectively conveyed.
It would be wise for me to prepare myself and
listen to His words so that I can be
successful and learn.
By following His lead, I can become that positive
force, I can fight any problem on
any level of concern.
I pray that I will never second-guess myself when I
face the music or problems that are
caused by this land.
I pray that I will feel completely secured from
failure for my final decision will be under
my God's command.

Proverbs 19:21
There are many devices in a man's heart; nevertheless
the counsel of the LORD, that Shall stand———

A Prayer As A Poem—Richard A. Dixon

April 14

The Last Shall Be First

I pray on this day not to entertain the thought
about my rating by the world leaders
as being one of them.
In my heart I believe that my path takes a
difference way in life, it is that way of the
child borne in Bethlehem.
Although there were times that I concentrated on
the thought that my efforts should
have been rewarded.
Instead of coming up with some kind of recognition, the leaders overlooked me and my
bubble was bombarded.
I pray that my prime purpose is my best and I will
always keep my God in my heart
in all that I do.
I pray that I will never directly seek the material
world as my number one goal,
that is not my view.
I pray to do the right thing, and again to do my
best in doing His will, these are the
things in which I thirst.
I thank my God to know that I will remain pure in
heart for in heaven the last here
on earth will be first.

Matthew 19:30
But many of the first shall be last; and the last shall be first———

A Prayer As A Poem — Richard A. Dixon

April 15

Living By His Standards

On this day I pray to be guided by the virtues
of heaven that are characterized by
honesty and love.
It is only in the eternal value of my life that I
can live that quality life that will fit like
a spiritual glove.
I pray that my standards will come from the
spirit because it is in these that I gain the
virtue of being unselfish.
It is in these values that negatives cannot survive and the force of good will help me to
obtain my ultimate wish.
Living in this world we should constantly contribute to the things of values in
being our ultimate role.
I pray by living by the rules that are ordained
by our God that we are increasingly assured
of an eternal soul.

John 16:13
Howbeit when he, the spirit of truth, is come, he will guide into all truth———

A Prayer As A Poem — Richard A. Dixon

April 16

Never Give Up - Reach Out

Let me pray on this day that my heart will be filled
with that caring and sharing with all those
who cross my mind.
I pray that I will reach out to them and pray for
them and all the results and efforts
will be well-defined.
I pray that somehow and someway that I will
be able to make a difference to bring them
closer to our LORD.
I pray that I can help them to flame their divine
spark to shine within,
to show them their spiritual reward.
Even if I fail in my efforts to help someone to
build that light in their heart, I will
persevere and try again.
I am only God's messenger and that light in
time may develop because of that
message from deep within.
I pray that my prayers will be answered and that
my help will always be there as strong and as
tall as the tallest tower.
I pray that I will never weaken in my efforts to
reach out in my caring for that is the
goodness of my God's power.

Hebrews 4:16
Let us therefore boldly come into the throne of grace, that
we may obtain mercy, and find grace in time of need—

A Prayer As A Poem — Richard A. Dixon

April 17

The Unseen Are Forever

On this day I pray that I will not be a slave
to those earthly things that
I can now see.
I pray that I will never become emotionally
attached so that my soul will
always be free.
It is in what we see is what we get and they
are not made to withstand
the weight of time.
These things of the world have their limita-
tions and in the end their value
isn't worth a dime.
I pray that we will all come to
believe as it is written in the
bible for all to see.
That these universal things that we view every
day only last temporarily but the spirit of
God is for eternity.

2 Corinthians 4:18
While we look not at the things which are seen——— things which are seen are temporal but the things which are not seen are eternal.

A Prayer As A Poem — Richard A. Dixon

April 18

Fear The Loss Of Heaven Most of All

On this day let me pray that I will fear the
most the loss of heaven than anything that
might be in hell.
I pray that I will put my Almighty God above
everything that I know for heaven is the only
place I want to dwell.
I pray to put the world and all of its wonders
behind me when it comes to
putting my God first.
I pray that I will see all things that God offers
me for it is only His blessings that will keep
me from being cursed.
I pray that we all will put Our Almighty God
first in our minds for no matter what we do,
He will forgive.
I pray that this peace of mind beyond man's
understanding will be given to all so
that all may live.
I pray to see that it is things of the ordained
virtues of heaven that gives life and all
will see me through.
I pray that my will to do my LORD'S way
will now and always take precedence
in all that I do.

Psalm 19:9
The fear of the LORD is clean enduring Forever; the judgements of the LORD are true———

A Prayer As A Poem — Richard A. Dixon

April 19

Cleanse Our Souls And Confess Our Sins

I pray on this day that I will keep reminding
myself that Jesus washed
His Disciples' feet.
He got down on His knees and performed the
duties of a servant to assure their
lives to be complete.
This spiritual exercise was meant to be a symbol of cleansing the dirt of sin from
the souls of man.
This washing was also directed by Jesus to wash
one another's feet to help others in their
heart to understand.
I pray to know in the end that I will have to go
through my Lord savior Jesus when
I am dirty with sin.
And I pray to know that I cannot help others
until I have made peace with Jesus,
I must be born again.

John 13:14
If then your Lord and Master have washed your feet;
you also ought to wash one another feet———

A Prayer As A Poem — Richard A. Dixon

April 20

Preparing For The Beyond

On this day I pray that I will continue my
earnest prayers seeking all that is from
the heavens on high.
I pray that my doing for Him will positively
last and will be that striving force
until the day I die.
I pray that through my earnest
prayers my loving efforts will
be an eternal bond.
I pray that I will help glorify that moment
with my God when I pass
into that great beyond.
I pray that my last prayer to my God will be
an indication to my steps to glory was
the making of a holy gem.
I pray that everything in that prayer will be
an indication that my every purpose
was getting close to Him.
I pray that we all will reach down into our
souls and feed that divine spark that will
give us a spiritual plus.
I pray that the flame will become a light that
will show us all the way and will be a
shining beam for all of us.

Revelation 21:1
And I saw a new heaven and a new earth———

Thessalonians 4:16
For the LORD himself shall descend from heaven with a shout———

A Prayer As A Poem — Richard A. Dixon

April 21

We Should Agree On Earth

I pray on this day that my agreement with
others will be as it should be for
I am not God.
I pray that I will be able to live and let live
although our lives are a bit
different and at odds.
I know to be indifferent to those different
from me will only add fuel to
an explosive fire.
To take matters in my hands and insist they do
things the way that I do could create an
unforgivable hot wire.
I pray that we all can live together in harmony
and always show God's spirituality so that we
will never show any disrespect.
I pray that God will reinforce my positive attitude for my knowledge is limited and
my ways are not perfect.
I pray to see the whole picture and to let me
know that others are all equal under
God as a person.
I pray to be guided by the hand of God and
show tolerance so the situation
will not ever worsen.

Matthew 18:19
Again I say unto you, that if two of you shall on earth as———it shall be done for them———

A Prayer As A Poem — Richard A. Dixon

April 22

Not As A Fool But Wise

Let me pray on this day that I will go to my
LORD and ask Him to rid myself of all
emotional outrage.
I pray that I will not reside in the notion that just
because I am human I will be locked in
a negative cage.
I pray that we all come to the conclusion that
just because we now live as a fool doesn't
mean we should die a fool.
If we will come to our senses and pray for that
change we can be His emissary and begin
to use His spiritual tools.
I pray that we will all understand that our
actions are a direct result of who we
are and what's in the mind.
What really counts is what's in our hearts
and by coming to your God, He can make
those see who once were blind.

Ephesians 5:15
See them that walk circumspectly, not as a fool, but as wise———

A Prayer As A Poem — Richard A. Dixon

April 23

Honesty Is The Way Of God

**On this day I pray that all will join me in a
pledge that deceit will not be
apart of your heart.
Fibbing to the LORD is a serious offense and
He does not and will not allow it in His house,
it is a deadly dart.
It is terminally damaging to everything that
it touches, but most of all God does
not like dishonesty.
Lying tears down all of the virtues that our
heaven stands for, such as
trust and credibility.
I pray that we will understand that not telling
the truth rates very high on the
totem pole of sin.
It is written that people were struck down dead
for lying in the early days, be careful
this could happen again.
I pray that we can all see the joy and happiness
in putting all of His ways in
all of our affaires.
Being pure in heart we can be assured of
no problems in climbing
God's heavenly stairs.**

Roman 13:13
Let us walk honestly, as in the day, not in the rioting———

A Prayer As A Poem — Richard A. Dixon

April 24

The LORD Is Our Spiritual Place

I pray on this day that I will always be aware
where to go when this world gives me
more than I can bear.
I pray that I will always enter His Spiritual place
and begin to commune with Him
with my earnest prayers.
I pray that this knowledge of His open door
will be known to all so they can
find that peace.
It is indeed knowing that God is the only
one to see and to find that spiritual
ultimate release.
By coming to His spiritual place you will find
security and peace, the world's fears to
us will never be a threat.
It should be born and instilled in all of our
minds and pray that this is one thing
you should never forget.

Psalm 90:1
LORD thou have been our dwelling place In all generation———

A Prayer As A Poem — Richard A. Dixon

April 25

Show That Mercy That Was Given To You

On this day I pray that I will show
mercy to those who show
unkindness to me.
I pray that my kindness to them will be a seed
that will grow in them to let them know
love is the key.
To give mercy and to look for goodness in them
and adhere to the agreement that we
can peacefully disagree.
I pray to do this and to find that under-
standing no matter how rude
their words may be.
I pray that my LORD will allow me to see the
pain of those who are misbehaving because
of some personal problem.
I pray that my mercy will develop into a special
prayer to them so that one day they
will take it all to Him.
I pray that I will let the ways of my Savior
Jesus through me show that mercy so that
we all can religiously bond.
I pray that I will not allow the disease
of bad behavior to take roots
in the way that I respond.

Proverbs 16:6
by mercy and truth iniquity is purged: and———men
depart from evil———

A Prayer As A Poem—Richard A. Dixon

April 26

The Virtues Of Heaven Saves

On this day I pray that I will look again to things
like honesty and love to bring me closer to
my Lord Jesus' side.
I will not look to the world's possessions and its
recognition to find peace to make me
content and satisfied.
I pray as I have always strived to use unself-
ishness when it comes to others so that
we all can bond.
I will not seek fame, to be in the world's spotlight,
for true happiness cannot be found
in this magic wand.
I pray to put true love for all in everything
that I do, so that the spirit of
God will forever flow.
Material things could never save our souls or give
us true happiness, it's being pure in heart that
makes our lives glow.

John 14:17
Peace I leave with you, my peace I give unto you; not as the world giveth———

A Prayer As A Poem — Richard A. Dixon

April 27

Mind-Set Can Determine What You Expect

I pray on this day that my mind-set will be on
the same track as my LORD and
His purpose for us.
I pray that my mind-set will be a part of those
things and actions that will make our
lives a heavenly plus.
I pray because of my ways of thinking that I
always expect my spiritual life will
daily get better.
I pray that because of the way that I live that my
God sees that I am an active
spiritual go-getter.
We should all pray that we be all guided by our
God so that He can help us to develop
a righteous mind.
I pray that my mind will be set and dialed in on
all of His wills so that my efforts will be
definitely of His kind.

Philippians 4:7
And the peace of God, which pass all understanding, shall keep your hearts and minds through Christ———

A Prayer As A Poem — Richard A. Dixon

April 28

Never Give Up, Never Lose Faith

On this day I pray that I will experience the
better things in life in all of its sacred
goodness and worth.
I pray if trouble falls upon me that I will, with
God's help, withstand any force that comes
from this earth.
I pray if I have gotten into a corner
and I have found myself
down and out,
I pray that I will reach for that heavenly
strength that will turn my direction
completely about.
I pray that none of these things will happen, but
I must understand this world brings
heartaches and pain.
I pray as a believer in God and Jesus and I
everything will be all right as I hold onto
His spiritual reins.

Psalm 51:11
Do not take me away from your presence and your free spirit———

A Prayer As A Poem — Richard A. Dixon

April 29

We All Are Family

I pray on this day to be all that my God will
have me to be because of my position on
His family tree.
His spirit and blood runs through all of us, we
have been given the chance and gift to
live for eternity.
It is written in the bible that we have been
proclaimed in His holy degree, like Christ
as one of the heirs.
In God's family we are given the status similar
to angels and in heaven our movements
are unimpaired.
I pray that we can religiously see each of us
as walking Temples and each ordained as
a spiritual domicile.
I pray that we will raise our spiritual minds and
thoughts to the very highest as being His
most blessed child.

Matthew 6:9
Our Father which art in heaven, Hallowed be thy
name———

A Prayer As A Poem — Richard A. Dixon

April 30

You Should Prosper From Your Experiences

On this day I pray to react to all of my ex-
periences and make maximum use of
my God-given skills.
It is because of my diversified experiences
that I have survived and received
the gift to do His will.
I pray that I will forget the pain that I endured
during my tormented days, from these
memories I must withdraw.
I pray now to give all of that learning experience
away to others for now I am guided
by His Almighty's law.
I pray and recognize that I have been blessed
and given an abundance of grace because of
my efforts of giving to all.
I pray that all will come to know that it is in
giving that you receive His blessing
right up to your final call.

Luke 6:38
Give and it shall be given unto you; good measure———

A Prayer As A Poem — Richard A. Dixon

May 1

Serve - As In Serve The LORD

This day I pray that I will serve my
God in some way that He
will have me to.
I pray that I will listen well to His voice in
order that I might be right
in whatever I do.
It is well accepted that all of us have that
unique purpose to serve our Almighty
in some special way.
I pray that we will all find that purpose
and recognize the opportunity to
help and obey.
I pray that we will understand that our Lord
will not assign us to a project that
we cannot fulfill or like.
All of our hearts are in one accord when it comes to
caring, and we have no fears, not even
when His thunder strikes.
I pray that I will take this privilege and serve Him
by serving others in helping
whenever I can.
I pray others will join with me in fulfilling
and completing our Almighty's
perfect spiritual plan.

Colossians 3:24
Knowing that of the LORD you shall receive the rewards
of the inheritance for you have served the Lord———

A Prayer As A Poem—Richard A. Dixon

May 2

Continuation In Prayer Gives You Strength

This day I pray that I will never forget
the magnitude of power in
prayer to fight sin.
I pray that I will be forever aware that there
is no communication more important
than talking to Him.
By coming to Him in prayer at any time, I know
that He will be listening to what I am saying
to Him from my heart.
There should be no concern about Him missing a
single word you say for He is waiting for
you even before you start.
Our Almighty tells us that prayer is a part of that
lifeline that connects our souls to Him and
it's always one on one.
There is nothing here on earth that could equal
the power, its effectiveness in getting
the right things done.
I pray that I will always see that prayer is a
God-giving way to survive just as
breathing in His air.
It is in prayer that you receive strength in doing
His will and the path to eternal life that
He so gladly shares.

Act 6:4
But we will give ourselves continually to Prayer, and to the ministry———

A Prayer As A Poem—Richard A. Dixon

May 3

We Are A Sacrificing Temple

This day I pray that it will remain born in
the mind that my body and soul is a
temple for God as man.
I pray that I will do all those things to keep
it from harm and make it even
better whenever I can.
Our Almighty has created us in His image and
He has raised us on a pedestal to a
value being most high.
We should respond in kind by doing His will
and live as His temple and to
this we should glorify.
Our faith tells us, and it is written, that we will
have an eternal body but there
will be some change.
Things will be significant y different because He
will rid us of all of those things
that were deranged.
I pray that I will understand that when I go against
His will I will bring some damage to the temple,
I don't want to offend.
I pray that I will forever know that this body
is His temple, it does not belong to me, for
it all belongs to Him.

Roman 12:11
Beseech you therefore, brethren by the mercy of God,
that you present your bodies a living sacrifice————

A Prayer As A Poem — Richard A. Dixon

May 4

Truly Believing In Him

On this day I pray that God can truly change
everything in life and He can
truly make it good.
I pray that I will persevere and continue to
believe so that one day all of His work
will be understood.
Thank God, I have seen others who have become
blessed through their faith and
who have strive earnestly.
They have found that inner peace and that miraculous change through His grace
for the world to see.
I pray that all will someday take up this belief
and find that path that leads away
from the wrath of sin.
This is where they will find nothing but serenity, love, happiness, and joy in
heaven by being with Him.
I pray in all of my prayers that I will forever
hold onto believing and doing what my
Almighty will have me to do.
I pray by keeping my trust in Him, I will become that light to show others and make
their life gloriously brand-new.

Galatians 3:22
The scripture says all who are with sin, the promise by faith of Jesus Christ might be given to them that believe———

A Prayer As A Poem — Richard A. Dixon

May 5

His Spirit And Our Will Power

On this day I pray that I will be given the
knowledge and ability to accept God's
free will as a gift.
My heart and soul tell me to give all a helping
hand and with His strength I will
receive a spiritual lift.
I pray that I will be humbly thankful and show
my gratitude by caring for others and giving
them a spiritual nudge.
I pray that I will utilize my righteous ways and
glorify my unselfishness and
let God be my judge.
I pray that I will not be hesitant in using my
free will to think God will
see me through.
I pray that I will forever stay on that road
in helping others so that I
will forever endue.

PHILIPPIANS 2:13
For it is God that works in you both to will and to do of
His good———

A Prayer As A Poem — Richard A. Dixon

May 6

We Should Follow God In His Caring

This day I pray to put foremost in my mind
to open up to my fellowman to let
them know that I care.
I will pray that in my efforts to make the point
by doing the right things and to help and
keep them from despair.
I pray that I will be there when
they need a word to inspire
them along the way.
I pray that God will put those
words in my heart in
everything that I say.
Many times we take it for granted and we do
not tell especially our loves ones
exactly how we feel.
I pray that on this day I will talk to them and
open my heart and let them know that
I care and always will.

1Peter 5:7
Casting all your cares upon Him; for He cares for you———

A Prayer As A Poem — Richard A. Dixon

May 7

Come To Him And Receive His Goodness

This day I pray that I will not do anything
that will hinder my LORD's spirit to
flow in and through me.
I pray that His flow will continuously run
through my soul to assure me and
make me sinful free.
It is the power of my Almighty that will give me
that strength to be active in
carrying out His plan.
I am praying that my efforts will not be any
distraction but will be a booster in
being a helping hand.
I pray that I will be as a child and accept whatever comes what may, and be what my God
will have me to be.
I pray that I will be obedience to the end so that
I will be given His blessings
through His holy decree.

Matthew 11:23
Come unto me all you that labor and are heavy laden and
I will give you rest———

A Prayer As A Poem — Richard A. Dixon

May 8

An Understanding Heart

On this day I pray that I will not be the one
that will over reacts and respond
negatively to others.
I pray that my remarks will be kind in meaning
and that I will show compassion to
my sisters and brothers.
As humans it is not unusual that we may get a
little upset when something is said or
done that we don't like.
If we talk without thinking, we instantly set up a
defense by fighting fire with fire and sometimes
do things for spite.
I pray that my heart will be so full of love and
understanding that it will prevent what
could become a fight.
I pray that my beliefs and my Almighty will give
me the knowledge and direction and
turn evil into a right.
I pray that others will see in me that God
is indeed in my heart as I live
and walk on this land.
It is only my God that I depend on and to pray
to help me in all of my situations for
my hand is in His hand.

Psalm 119:169
Let my cry come near before thee O LORD: give me
understanding according to thou word———

A Prayer As A Poem — Richard A. Dixon

May 9

Say No To Negative Pride

**On this day I pray that I will never let negative
pride stand in the way and keep me
from what is right.
I pray that I will always continue to be firmly humble so that my God's spirit will flow freely
both day and night.
I pray that I will not be so proud to speak to
those who may be less fortunate and
seem totally down.
I pray to God to show me the way to reach out
to them and help, but never by
showing them a frown.
I pray not to be that person that will give others
the impression and reason that I am
so much within myself.
I pray that God will take away all my selfish
pride in my heart and allow
only LOVE to be left.**

1Samuel 2:3
Talk no more so exceedingly proud; let not arrogance come out of your mouth———

A Prayer As A Poem — Richard A. Dixon

May 10

Start By Looking In The Right Places

This day I pray that I will not look in all of
those places that harbor wrong to assist
me in finding my way.
I pray that I will also realize that first I cannot
become stable by being indecisive in my
quest from day to day.
I pray that I will know what to do and where
to find help that will get me back
where I belong.
I pray that the doors of my heart and soul will
remain open so that God's spirit can enter
to keep me strong.
Living in this world, we all will need assistance
sometimes and to succeed we
must look from within.
I pray that we will always seek the religious
virtues though we can't see them, we feel
that power when we win.
To find peace of mind and that ultimate serenity, do not look in the material places, it's
too much of an odd.
I pray that we start by focusing on our hearts
and souls for the healing can only come
from the grace of God.

Psalm 90:1
LORD thou has been our dwelling place in all generation———

A Prayer As A Poem—Richard A. Dixon

May 11

There Is Nothing Like A Mother's Love

On this day I pray especially for the creation of
all mothers living and those whom have
passed into the hereafter.
By the grace of God all mothers have been
given a gift that is only for them, that
motherly love and laughter.
True motherly love cannot be equal and
it can be seen because of
its radiant beam.
This purpose in life has been made for
them to maintain our God's
love and esteem.
I pray and give thanks to MARY
for being the one for God's
heaven-given conception.
Only God could create this manifestation
to give us a way to eternal salvation
without any exceptions.

John 2:5
His (Jesus) mother said unto the servants, whatsoever He says unto you do it———

A Prayer As A Poem — Richard A. Dixon

May 12

A Kingdom Without Sin

On this day I pray that we will come face to
face on just how much sin has infiltrated
our world's factions.
We all must come to that mental awareness
that we all sin to some degree in our daily
thoughts and actions.
No matter how much we may minimize the sin
that's in our mind, when we judge someone
harshly on what they say.
To even think negative of others in any small
degree is wrong in God's eyes for this is
not what His heart displays.
I pray that we can be more conscious of our
selfishness with our love ones when we act
and say things wrong.
Being insensitive, dogmatic, untrustworthy
are just scratching the surface, in what
we can do all day long.
Let us all pray to do better and see His kingdom and His love and let us make it a rule
to work with our divine spark.
Let us all pray and be spiritualize by His
Grace, and let us all care for each other
by being pure in heart.

2Timothy 4:18
And the LORD shall deliver me from every evil work, and will preserve me unto His heavenly kingdom; to be whom be glory forever———

A Prayer As A Poem — Richard A. Dixon

May 13

We Will Carry His Banner

This day I pray I will carry the banner that
will give me that comforting feeling that we
all are God's children.
I pray that I will reinforce that privilege and
belief by doing His will and being one
of His devoted pilgrims.
I pray that I will do my part and consistently
recognize that my LORD is always
in my presence.
The thought of my consciousness of Him will
give me that necessary confidence of
feeling joyfully pleasance.
Life will also be a disaster if we did have belief
in our fellowman for we can ot live
in this world alone.
We all must pray for each other more to maintain
our spiritual bond otherwise things
will go so wrong.
I pray that we will find the love and caring that
we receive from God by believing in Him and
making Him our choice.
I pray that we will listen to Him by connecting
to His lifeline so that we will forever hear His
glorious comforting voice.

Psalm 20:5
We will rejoice in thy salvation, and in the name of our
God we will set up our banners———

A Prayer As A Poem—Richard A. Dixon

May 14

Making Things Right That Once Were Wrong

On this day I pray that I will not be victimized
by arrogance and the results that
it can give me.
Being self-centered will hinder reality and taking
the problem out of His hands could
hamper my morality.
I pray that I will seek always the counsel of my
LORD in my course of making plans
of material possessions.
If I did not go to Him and put ownership first in
my mind, the love of these things might
become an obsession.
If you become deeply in love with the material,
it could become a bad mistake and a hazard
to your happiness.
In the end you will find that you can't find real
love in things you own, you only
find lonely emptiness.
I pray that I will not be tempted and controlled
by these passions that can bring you no more
than a brief dream.
I pray that I will always have my priorities right
by following that light that shines from
God's heavenly beam.

1Timothy 6:11
But thou O man of God————follow after Righteousness,
godliness, faith, love, patience, meekness—

A Prayer As A Poem—Richard A. Dixon

May 15

The Law Of Spirituality

On this day I pray that I will improve my
development in the spirit
of all things.
I pray that I will acknowledge in doing so
that I will be following the laws of my
king of kings.
I know that if I continue to grow in spirit
everyday, my way will become more
and more like His way.
I will be able to see more of His love in life
and I will find more answers in caring
that will be on display.
I pray on this day that I will not be the
ailment but be the resolve that
will make things right.
I know by following these spiritual laws
I will be of the plan that will make my
future loving and bright.
I pray that I will find that meaning of why I
am here so that I can do my part
and to make it right for all.
I pray that all of my actions will follow His
law until my God Almighty makes to me
that final and last call.

Psalm 119:174
I have longed for thy salvation, O LORD. and thy law is my delight———

A Prayer As A Poem — Richard A. Dixon

May 16

Do Not Forget To Remember

On this day I pray to remember when negatives
enter my mind and my actions
respond in the same,
I pray that I will stop immediately and remember to ask my God for guidance so that my
good can be reclaimed.
I pray not to forget when selfishness tries to
take control of me and make me think
I am the center of all.
I pray to ask God to come into my mind and direct my thoughts back to being sensitive and
tear down my selfish wall.
To remember our LORD in these important
times of need will be the right thing to do
in order to fulfill His will.
We should pray to always come to Him to give
us His gift of love and he will teach us never
to forget Him now and until.

Psalm 78:7
That they might set their hope in God and not to forget the works of God———

A Prayer As A Poem — Richard A. Dixon

May 17

To Save Yourself And Others

This day I pray that in our life we should be
aware of the paradox, to give up your
lives you can save them.
When you sit back, taking the route of playing
it safe, you will find emptiness and to
this you will be condemned.
I pray that we can see the joy in sharing
your life with others giving them
your help and time.
I pray that we can foresee that by caring for
others we gain strength to help others
to make that positive climb.
It is not how long we live but how we live that
will give spiritual meaning to make
our lives a divine plus.
I pray that we will live guided by our God so
that the goodness of all will be
shared by all of us.
If we only focus on those things of the
world to live that life, it is
not the way to go.
To live for the world alone you will jeopardize
your spiritual world and forfeit
to live forever more.

Hebrew 7:25
Wherefore he is able to save them to the utter upmost
that come unto God———

A Prayer As A Poem — Richard A. Dixon

May 18

Learn From Your Experiences

On this day I pray to react with an open mind
to all of my experiences and welcome
its testing drill.
It is because of His grace and strength that
I will make that climb no matter how
steep the hill.
I pray that I will forget the pain that I endured
during my tormented days, from these
memories I must withdraw.
I pray now to give the blessings that I receive
from this to others for then I'm blessed again
for this is His spiritual law.
I pray that in following His way it will ordain
my faith because of my efforts
of giving to all.
I pray to know that I will continue to receive
His blessings for this is His everlasting
spiritual protocol.

Luke 6:38
Give and it shall be given unto you———

A Prayer As A Poem — Richard A. Dixon

May 19

Fight That Good Fight Of Faith

This day I pray to be reminded of all of those
negative forces that are eliminated by our
counter forces of good conveyers.
These counter actions are illustrated throughout
the bible in its writings, let us mention
some in our prayer.
I pray when I find discord that I will use my
spiritual knowledge and replace it
with spiritual order.
I pray that when I see bad things I will provide
good and take my fellowman from
that evil, evil border.
When others find themselves so deep in trouble,
I pray my God will help me to build their faith
and strength to carry on.
I pray that I will always be able to make every-
one better by showing them love instead
of hate until all evil is gone.

1Timothy 6:12
Fight that good fight of faith, lay hold to eternal life———

A Prayer As A Poem — Richard A. Dixon

May 20

Lifted Out Of The Darkness

On this day I pray and thank my God for all
of the bad things that He has taken
out of my heart and soul.
I pray and thank my God again that I do not
miss them in the least for I have been
lifted out of a deep hole.
I thank God that I can see clearly the light that
shines on the road that I must travel to
reach the promised land.
I thank Him now that I can stand and walk
with the strength that I have received from
the power of His hands.
It is now that I pray to my God, my faith
and trust in Him that I live with
heaven in my heart.
I pray and thank my God for I have found
ultimate joy, for my heaven on earth
has gotten its start.

James 1:21
Wherefore lay apart all filthiness — — —
and receive with meekness the engrafted word, which is able to save your soul———

A Prayer As A Poem — Richard A. Dixon

May 21

Stop And Talk With Him

I pray on this day that when I get that uneasiness
and feel that something inside me
should not be there.
I pray that I will stop and commune with my
LORD so that I will rid myself of fear
and will not despair.
I pray to God that I will not try to fight the
demons by myself for that will be
blundering and absurd.
I pray that I will stop and listen to
Him for I need to be guided
and heavenly spurred.
At times we all get that something in our hearts
and block out God, then we
start to worry.
At this time we should use discipline and tell
ourselves to be still for we get too much
in a hurry.
I will stop and listen for His voice and feel His
presence and open up my heart and
let Him come within.
I pray to commune with my Lord Jesus, and ask
for guidance so He will rid me
of my worries and sin.

Psalm 46:10
Be still and know that I am God: I will be exalted among the heathen———

A Prayer As A Poem — Richard A. Dixon

May 22

Love Leads To The Eternal Hate Leads To Darkness

On this day I pray that I will never be a
carrier of hatred in any way, any
form, or any degree.
I pray that I will be able to crust it with love so
that my freedom from it will be
a sacred guarantee.
Living a life of hate is indeed not living at all
for real life cannot survive when there
is no rationalization.
Our world is so complex and it is a fact that hate
is a main reason why there are wars
between the nations.
I pray that all would use their 20/20 hindsight
that no one is a winner when we engage
in the works of devilment.
I pray that unselfishness and most of all love
will prevail so that fulfilling His word lives
on with spiritual confidence.

Proverbs 10:12
Hatred stirred up strife: but love covereth all sin———

A Prayer As A Poem — Richard A. Dixon

May 23

Developing Through GOD

**On this day I pray and thank my LORD for
protecting me while I went through my
developing days.
At times my life was tormented by self-inflicted
mistakes because of my
irrational ways.
I pray now that I know that there are certain
things that can't be taught by just words or
by sitting in a class.
It is only through personal experience that your
bell is rung and you can see that
light at long last.
I pray now that my God will continue to give me
that spiritual power and guidance
to walk in His light.
I pray forever that He will be my spiritual
teacher for my heart is open to do the
things that are right.**

**Psalm 25:4and 5
Show me your way LORD and teach me your way—-
Lead me in your truth and teach me———**

A Prayer As A Poem—Richard A. Dixon

May 24

Repent And Fight The Evil

I pray on this day that my going and coming will
not be infested by the turmoil and
its evil fragments.
I pray not to be that misled person who will
allow anger to enter my heart to
cause discontentment.
I pray when I pass any corner that I will not
give hate the time of day to
avoid any danger.
I will keep my eyes on the spirit of my LORD, I
will then be able to repent the evil of
that stranger.
Wherever I am challenged with doubt of what
to do I will pray and put it in His hands
and I will be still.
I know and pray by trusting and keeping the
faith in Him I will receive grace to do the
fullness of His will.

Matthew 3:2
And saying repent you: for the kingdom of heaven———

A Prayer As A Poem — Richard A. Dixon

May 25

Commit To His Way

On this day I pray that I will not concern
myself or my mind about the surface of
things that happens to me.
I pray that I will commit completely to His
word for doing it His way will help me
fight the things of misery.
Love, peace, purity will bring safety to my home
and warm my heart for the spirit of
God will always flow.
These glorious blessings will keep my faith no
matter what or how many times
the rooster may crow.
I pray that my indisputable consistency in
depending on all of those spiritual traits
will stay in my soul.
I pray to remain His channel for in doing I
will be forever blessed and I will be
under His complete control.

Psalm 37:5
Commit thy way unto the LORD, trust always in Him———

A Prayer As A Poem—Richard A. Dixon

May 26

Increase Your Spiritual Knowledge

I pray on this day that I will be able to go
further in doing well for others that will
be what my God will wants.
It is not God's way to live on yesterday's deeds
to sit on the fence and have that
air of being nonchalant.
I pray to progress from day to day by listening
to my Almighty for He is always
in my presence.
I know that my attentiveness to His words
will destroy the devil-work, with His
love and diligence.
I pray to continue to broaden my spiritual
knowledge so that I will not be restricted in
learning about the unknown.
I pray that someday that I will reach that point
toward perfection to let God see that
I have truly spiritually grown.

Colossians 1:10
That you might walk worthy of the LORD———and increasing in the knowledge of the LORD.

A Prayer As A Poem—Richard A. Dixon

May 27

We All Need That Spiritual Awakening

On this day I pray that I will always be
grateful for my spiritual awakening
that God placed in my soul.
I may not know that exact moment that the
blessing came to me but it is the most
important that I will uphold.
I pray that all will realize that the most important relationship in our lives is the
relationship with our creator.
We should also realize that it is from His kingdom that we do worldly good by making
Him our spiritual navigator.
I pray to know that I took the right path and my
Almighty has given me His grace and love to
fight turmoil and strife.
I pray for all to ask our Lord Jesus to forgive
us for our sins for He died for our sins so that
we can have eternal life.

1Corinthians 15:34
Awake to righteousness and sin not; for some have not the knowledge of God———

A Prayer As A Poem — Richard A. Dixon

May 28

Concern Yourself Not But Face What The Day May Bring

I pray on this day that I will not lose faith
although the day may be coupled
with pressing problems.
I pray that I will not miss a step in continuing
my walk by His side for He is the
holy child of Bethlehem.
I pray to continue to remain a believer and to
keep my heart and soul open so that I will
continue to receive His heavenly flow.
I know that my LORD will take care of my worries
and my tormented valleys will be brought to
the height of a glorious chateau.
I pray to know that my days will get better from
day to day as long as I keep my
life under His care.
I pray now to take full advantage of this
opportunity to help glorify this time
with this earnest prayer.

Proverbs 27:1
Boast not thyself————for thou know not what a day may bring forth————

A Prayer As A Poem — Richard A. Dixon

May 29

His Mercy Will Bring You Back

On this day I pray that I will forever acknow-
ledge that my God is merciful and forgiving
for all of His believers.
I pray and know that He will always show us
His mercy even though we may be
consistent under achievers.
I pray to know that no matter how far we may
fall away from Him He will bless us and
guide us back to His path.
Sometimes before we ask for mercy He searches
our heart and gives us that mercy
inspite of our sinful wrath.
I pray that my faith will be strengthened and
my trust in Him will be stronger
than ever before.
I pray that in accepting the fact that my God
always welcomes us back through
His merciful door.

Matthew 5:7
Blessed are the merciful: for they shall obtain mercy—

A Prayer As A Poem — Richard A. Dixon

May 30

One Prayer A Day To Keep Sin Away

On this day I pray that I will include the power
of prayer, covering my caring for the world,
praying that we all benefit.
I pray that each day I will take time out at least
once to pray for all to become
spiritually close knit.
If only there were significantly more of us that
would take a few moments out of their day to
pray for the goodness of all.
We will see the power of prayer would indeed
bring us closer to peace and bring
down those dividing walls.
I pray to persevere to do my part each day to
pray for the betterment of our world so
all will find that peace.
I pray that we will all pray that we will put the
Almighty in control so that the goodness
of our lives will increase.

Psalm 55:17
Evening, morning and at noon will I pray————And He shall hear my voice————

A Prayer As A Poem — Richard A. Dixon

May 31

Not Almost All - But All

I pray on this day that I will not just
give a portion of myself to God
in doing His will.
I pray that we all will understand that we
must bring it all to Him to succeed in
making our holy life real.
Some of us refuse to let go of some of our negative ways regardless of our conscious,
they do this without shame.
The excuses they give may be more of a denial
of the truth but they must face reality
for they are the blame.
Coming to God is like the ordained marriage
sanctioned by Him that you must give all to
complete that spiritual bond.
I pray that we will see that there are no options
in saving our souls for we must give all to enter
that ultimate glorious beyond.

Matthew 22:37
"THOU SHALL LOVE THE LORD THY GOD WITH ALL OF THY HEART, AND WITH ALL OF THY SOUL, AND WITH ALL OF THY MIND".

A Prayer As A Poem — Richard A. Dixon

June 1

It Is Better To Give And Be Blessed

I pray on this day that I will be
able to comfort someone
if only it's just a word.
I pray that this person will be lifted to a
spiritual high through me as a channel
from the divine third.
I pray to know that each time I find
within myself to think and to
do the right thing.
I pray to know that I will be making a payment
in the Almighty's sacred bank to
secure my angel's wings.
I will exercise my free will to do His will and
to help all that walk on
the face of this land.
I pray daily to receive His glorious gift by
giving my heart daily to complete His
glorious master plan.

Act 20:33
It is more blessed to give than to receive———

A Prayer As A Poem — Richard A. Dixon

June 2

It Starts With How You Think

I pray on this day that I will conceive that
what I really do in my actions start
with how I really think.
The rule starts with what's in your heart and soul
and will dictate my actions because
of their conscious link.
I pray that I will be that honest believer and
a consistent listener to all that
my God has to say.
I will know then that my mind will be filled with
His words and my actions
will be done His way.
I pray that with my spiritual devotion that my
conscious to my unconscious down to my soul
will be filled with love.
It will be then that my God will reside in my
heart and I will do all what's
done in heaven above.

Proverbs 23:7
For as he think in his heart, so is he———

A Prayer As A Poem — Richard A. Dixon

June 3

Every God Given Moment

On this day I pray that I will be what
my to be God will have me
every single moment.
I pray that I will regard each moment as a
God-given moment as being
spiritually well spent.
I pray to be aware that my God wants me to
primarily occupy myself with the presence,
I should focus on living in the now.
When focusing on the now, I will find fulfillment
in the search for answers, these will be just
some of the pluses that I will endow.
I pray to live in the moment and to give to
every moment what God
has given to me to give.
I pray that my mere presence will be that
spiritual force to better the future
for all of us to live.

Philippians 4:4
Rejoice in the LORD always and again I say, rejoice—

A Prayer As A Poem — Richard A. Dixon

June 4

Seeing All Of The Goodness For All

On this day I pray that I will see clearly all
of the virtues that will direct our lives
for the good of all.
I pray to take all of these virtues into my heart
and to transfer them into positive actions so
together we will stand tall.
It is in numbers that we can succeed and with-
stand the negatives of the world that
will cause us to divide.
I pray that we will all see that the goodness of
our being in one accord will give us
that reason to survive.
Thinking and sharing and giving with one
purpose in mind to love one another
and to build a spiritual team.
I pray that when we reach the hereafter that we
all can say we came together on earth
by His spiritual means.

1Peter 3:8
Finally be you all of one mind, having compassion one of another———

A Prayer As A Poem — Richard A. Dixon

June 5

The Master Plan In His Hands

I pray on this day that I will be joyful
because of my LORD'S plan and he
only knows it all.
I pray that I will not be bothered by the future
of His plan that may have me
to stumble or fall.
I pray that He will always give me that
strength no matter how tough
the storm may get.
I pray to know that my LORD will always be
there with me and real harm to me
will be no threat.
I pray to know that sooner than later my time
will come and the wind will blow my way and
push me in a better path.
I pray to know that my God has already written
my life and with Him in my heart I can
withstand the Devil's wrath.
I pray that all of us will continue to keep the
faith and trust in Him for all of our lives are
apart of His master plan.
I pray to keep our lives in His hands so that
ultimate joy will be ours in heaven
for every woman and man.

2 Samuel 22:31
As for God, His way is perfect———

A Prayer As A Poem — Richard A. Dixon

June 6

Fear The Loss Of Heaven

I pray on this day if I am going to put fear in
my life let that fear be the fear of my loss of
my God's kingdom and love.
I pray forever to be reminded by this positive
fear, this positive thought for I value most
what comes from above.
I pray that I will not confuse myself with the
negative fears that will bring strife
and close my heart.
I pray that my God's grace will be my guide-
line to keep my heart open, let these be
my working counterparts.
I pray to know what evil brings for we have all
been there, to lose the joy of heaven will be the
ultimate loss for all of us.
I believe that nothing can compare being in a
world of love, honesty, unselfishness for these
are all a God given plus.

Proverbs 3:7
Be not wise in your own eyes, fear the LORD, and depart from evil———

A Prayer As A Poem — Richard A. Dixon

June 7

People Like You And People Like Me

I pray on this day, O God, that people like
me will understand that we are no
better than any one else.
I pray that I will not say, "people like you",
because it is a phrase that put
others on an isolated shelf.
I pray to know that we all show signs of not
being perfect, into each of our lives
rain must fall.
We suffer pain, we have our moments, of failure
we respond negatively and we build
a selfish wall.
There is only one way to help each other and that
is to reach out to each other with
God's hand as the key.
We can pray together and work together and
have heaven on earth made by people like
you and people like me.

Proverbs 1:14
Cast in thy lot among us: let us all have one purse———

Proverbs 16:7
When a man's ways please the LORD, he make even
his enemies to be at peace with him———

A Prayer As A Poem—Richard A. Dixon

June 8

I Pray To Be Worthy

On this day I pray that when I am asked why do
I pray to my God I will say, "it is only because
of Him that I live".
Some would want to know why do I lend a hand
to help others and the answer is," I receive His
blessing when I give".
I pray to answer all of the questions that mankind put to me for I want all to know that one
day I will live in His home.
I pray to inform all of the unlearned that they
can find eternal peace if they follow the
path that leads to God's dome.
Knowing Him, Loving Him, and becoming a believer will give you the resolve that all will be
worth all of your efforts.
I pray that all will learn that He will bless you,
protect you, and guide you and then you will
have His eternal support.

Colossians 1:10
That you might walk worthy of the LORD unto all pleasing, being fruitful in every good works———

A Prayer As A Poem — Richard A. Dixon

June 9

Living And Being In The Spirit

I pray on this day to maintain that
life to live in the spirit
of the LORD.
I pray that with this spirit I will do
what a Christian does by
walking on toward.
Whatever this life may bring me, I
know I will prevail because of
His gift to me.
To be worthy of His grace, I will pass
His spirit onto others as one of
His devout appointees.
I pray whether I am having my lows in life
or my highs, I will not falter and
I will have no fear.
I will be holding the hand of my God and
His spirit will bond me and
I will forever persevere.

Roman 8:2 and 16
For the laws of Jesus Christ have made me free—The spirit itself bears witness with our spirit———We are the children of God—

A Prayer As A Poem—Richard A. Dixon

June 10

Well Doings Will Keep The Soul

On this day I pray that my frailties will be
controlled by God and my problems,
He will resolve.
I pray that by my continuing to do well, the
godly things will be the reason that
I spiritually evolve.
I pray that I will not resort to my
earthly ways to do what
I think is right.
It is only through Him that everything can
be brought out of the dark and clearly
seen in the light.
When we place all of our trust and faith in the
Almighty, He gives us the grace
to carry on.
I pray that all of us will use this trusting
energy so all races can be ran
by Him and won.

1 Peter 4:19
Wherefore————to the will of God commit the keeping of the soul to Him in well doing as unto a faith creator————

A Prayer As A Poem — Richard A. Dixon

June 11

When The Lord Comes I Will Rejoice

On this day I pray as a Christian I will
not fear the day when this earth
comes to an end.
Because of my total belief in my God I
will persevere to do all things
that He intends.
I pray to be positive in my steps each day on
the grounds that He has prepared
me to walk.
I pray that my God will continue to give me His
grace and let me say His words
whenever I talk.
I pray to go forward with the force of His spirit
in my soul that will make me
holy and sin free.
I pray to rejoice with my Lord Savior Jesus Christ
for when He comes again we shall
live in the eternity.

1Peter 4:7
But the end of all things is at hand: be you therefore sober, and watch unto prayer———

Psalm 32:21
For our hearts shall rejoice in Him, for we trusted in His holy name———

A Prayer As A Poem — Richard A. Dixon

June 12

Open The Door When Opportunity Knocks

I pray on this day to not overlook the
daily fact that opportunity knocks
each new day.
I pray to sieze the moment and be cognizant
of the chance to be a part of
its main stay.
So many times we either hesitate or even
feel inferior to meet some
particular challenge.
Suddenly the door of opportunity closes, we
can't reopen the door and it's something
we can avenge.
I pray to my God that I will always be prepared
to accept any chance to assure the spirit
flows on and on.
I pray that I will be there to answer His knock
and with His grace I will proudly do what
has to be done.

Revelation 3:20
BEHOLD I STAND AT THE DOOR AND KNOCK: IF ANY MAN HEAR MY VOICE, OPEN THE DOOR, I WILL COME IN TO HIM———

A Prayer As A Poem—Richard A. Dixon

June 13

How We Value Others

On this day I pray that I will make sure
that I will know exactly what values
to uphold in life.
I pray not to focus on the wrong things that
might bring you fame and it will
also bring you strife.
Living and giving your life a real chance means
that you cannot live only for
yourself and succeed.
I pray that all of my directions will come
from my Almighty to let that
spiritual course proceed.
I pray to always look away from myself and bond
spiritually with all for we are God's children
as sisters and brothers.
I pray that we will see that in the end that in
selfishness we don't receive His blessings, it is in the
action of valuing others.

Leviticus 19:18
Thou shall not avenge————but you should love your neighbor as thyself.

A Prayer As A Poem—Richard A. Dixon

June 14

Pray For Fathers, For Love Of Family

I pray on this day that all fathers will find
that heavenly strength to continue their
love for the family.
I pray that the bond that the father makes will
complete their family structure to have
love for eternity.
In our world the father at home will bring things
of goodness and good things will happen,
as they should.
I pray that all fathers will find their resolve for
happiness and live in harmony with love
as God would.
I pray that all fathers will act as fathers and
spiritually build and let them walk together
for all to see.
Fatherly love is God's preference to complete every
family and if His will is done this is way
that it will be.

Proverbs 4:1
Here you children, the instruction of a father, and attend to know understanding———

A Prayer As A Poem — Richard A. Dixon

June 15

Earn A Place In His Kingdom

I pray on this day that I will receive my grace
from my LORD by at least doing
some righteous deed.
The abundance of grace that we receive is proportional more than our human efforts in
how we proceed.
I pray to know that we could never equal our efforts to everything that our God does for us
as we roam.
It is because of His mercy and His love and His
undying desire to bring us all back to
His heavenly home.
It would behoove us to know that our duties are
to be pure in heart and forever except His word
as our guide.
I pray to take His path that leads to His kingdom
that would be the decision to earn a place to sit
by His side.

Philippians 2:13
For it is God that work in you both to will and to do His good———

A Prayer As A Poem — Richard A. Dixon

June 16

Not My Will But God's Will Be Done

On this day I pray that whatever situation I am in I pray to have to
do God's will.
I pray to know that God's plan has been
written and my actions are only a part of
His testing drill.
I pray that I will not get so involved with myself and lose sight of what my God will
have me to do.
I pray that I will continue on His spiritual
thinking track for that will be that what
I want to pursue.
I pray that we should not forget that He is the
only reason why we are living in this world,
remember this at all times.
When I get down on my knees to pray, I will
make sure to amend my prayer and say let
thy will be done not mine.

Psalm 37:5
Commit thy way unto the LORD; trust also in Him———

A Prayer As A Poem — Richard A. Dixon

June 17

Watching All Of His Wonders

This day I pray and thank God again for having
me to witness the sunrise that helps warm
our hearts and hands.
I pray and marvel at the innocence of the sky
and when the clouds cover the blue it's just
cover the blue it's just apart of the plan.
Seeing and hearing God's power unleashed in the
storms and winds that can change quickly this
land as we know it.
Experiencing the tenderness of the blossoming
of a flower reinforces my faith and even
more when the moon is lit.
I pray up to my last breath to breathe in the
splendor of the stars my faith and even
from coast to coast.
I pray to know that God could only do this
creation for He is the Father, the Son,
and the Holy Ghost.

Ecclesiastes 12:1
Remember now thy creator in the days of thy youth——

A Prayer As A Poem — Richard A. Dixon

June 18

He Is The Spirit That Brings Us Together

I pray on this day to do my part in carrying
out all of my duties as a part of
the spiritual team.
It should be known that our LORD is our force
in succeeding in completing
our spiritual dream.
Some of us will be that part of the force that will
constantly remind each other of His word so
that it will live in all.
I pray that all will recognize the privilege
to join and to contribute to the team
whenever we are called.
I pray that we will remain believers and receive
His strength to fight sin and torment that
comes in a devil's storm.
Living with God in His world makes us all
connected as one as the greatest team
to ever to be formed.

Matthew 18:20
FOR WHERE THERE ARE TWO OR THREE
GATHERED TOGETHER IN MY NAME, THERE AM
I———

A Prayer As A Poem—Richard A. Dixon

June 19

Thinking Of Yourself Could Be Harmful

I pray on this day to strive to eliminate my
selfish concerns or interests that block out
the welfare of others.
I pray that I will look away from myself and
search for the needs that are voiced by
the heart of another.
I pray that by taking that selfishness out of my
being I will be unimpaired in helping
the right things start.
I will not concern myself with the chances of not
being rewarded for my personal interest faction
has left my heart.
It is only that selfishness that gives you that exploited false belief and feelings hurt that you
are used only as a pawn.
I pray for the importance to know that it is not
so much what happens to me as long
as the right thing is done.

Roman 12:3
For I say, through the grace given to me———Not to think
of himself more highly than he ought to think———

A Prayer As A Poem — Richard A. Dixon

June 20

Fight To Give What You Have Received

I pray on this day that if I find someone
faced with the evil of darkness let me
be that channel to give them light.
If there is someone that is so deep in their
wrong let the word given to me by my
God make those wrongs right.
I pray if there is someone who is going back
ward let me be that guiding instrument to
help him or her make a turn-a-bout.
I pray also if I should find a fellowman that
is lost in a troublesome place let me be that
helping hand that pulls them out.
I pray that if someone thinks that it is only the
material world that counts, in God's world
is what you should believe.
If someone thinks it is best to keep what they ob-
tain for themselves let them know God's way,
it is better to give than receive.

2 Corinthians 9:7
Every man according to his purpose in his heart so let him give———for God loves a cheerful giver———

A Prayer As A Poem — Richard A. Dixon

June 21

God Is Reaching Out For Your Hand

I pray on this day that as I will walk on the
face of this earth I will graft His hand
that is reaching for mine.
I will do this with complete confidence know-
ing that our hearts will meet and
we will gloriously intertwine.
I pray by being with my heavenly father it
shows others how He will help us with
our problems from day to day.
By being by His side that He will be not only our
eyes and ears, but also His decisions for us will
keep us from going astray.
I pray that collectively we will all reach out our
hands and join with Him and form that
elite righteous congregation.
Coming together with this chain of faith we will
strengthen our virtues and build
an unbreakable foundation.

James 4:10
Humble yourself in the sight of the LORD and He shall
lift you up———

A Prayer As A Poem — Richard A. Dixon

June 22

Walking And Traveling His Road

On this day I pray again to remember that
the road that leads to God may start
as stony and hilly plaines.
But the more I travel that rough road it be
comes less troublesome and the ground
changes into a smooth level lane.
I pray to forever remember that my journey
may have started in complete darkness
without any source of light.
As soon as I took a step holding the hand of my
Lord Jesus everything around me suddenly
became progressively bright.
When I started moving up that road I did not
know or have many answers but my faith
guided me through everyday.
Now I have increased my knowledge much and I
now follow that beam of light in my soul that
leads to God's kingdom way.

2 Corinthians 5:7
For we walk by faith not by sight———

A Prayer As A Poem — Richard A. Dixon

June 23

Enjoy The Empowerment Of God

I pray on this day to empower and
utilize the spirit that comes
from Him to me.
I pray that His every word will enter my
heart and place my heart in tune of
being heavenly free.
Let the stream of goodness take complete
control of my spirit and take it to
the heavens high.
Let His love give me that power so that
I can share it with all so that
we all can fly.
I pray my encounter with Him today will give
me the walk that indicates that I am
walking towards Him.
I pray that others will join me as the three wise
men joined in walking and guided by
the star of Bethlehem.

Colossians 2:6
As you have therefore received in Christ Jesusthe LORD,
so walk you in Him———

A Prayer As A Poem—Richard A. Dixon

June 24

Let God's Work Appear In All

I pray on this day that everything that I do will
be relevant to His principles and
His moral laws.
Those who are a stranger to the works of the
LORD and when they finally see it, they
find it to be in awe.
The outsiders who become insiders will see as
believers that He can replace that
bitter chaos with order.
The now newly believers will find peace of mind
when they cross over from that
wrong side of the border.
I pray that we will all see that the believer will
find hope although they suffer from what
the world has brought.
I pray to keep the faith and trust in the Almighty
that love and caring will always
be the virtues we sought.

Psalm 90:16
Let thy work appear into thy servants and thy glory into unto their children———

A Prayer As A Poem — Richard A. Dixon

June 25

May All Of Our Hearts Come Together

I pray on this day that when I walk with my
fellowman that we be on that path that
leads to the kingdom on high.
I pray that when I talk to my fellowman that all
of our words are coming from
the same heavenly supply.
I pray that the eyes that I look into will rein
force my faith so that all of us will remain
in the goodness of His word.
We must all be cognizant of the fact that all of
this goodness comes to us because of
the grace of our divine third.
I pray when we all hold hands that we are
coming together in one accord and
we will be strong and true.
When we all walk by His side and take His
hand, we will be given eternal life as
believers of His righteous crew.

Colossians 2:2
That their hearts might be comforted, being knit together in love————to the acknowledgement of the mystery of God, and of the Father, and of Christ—

A Prayer As A Poem — Richard A. Dixon

June 26

An Evolution That Ends In A Positive Resolution

I pray on this day my soulful frailties will
work from head through my body, to
my feet and to the ground.
I pray then that I will use these frailties to walk
on and by doing so they will be crusted
into little small dust mounds.
I pray to rid of all of these weaknesses because
it seems that I cannot control these negatives
that come from my head.
It seems they have a mind of their own, these negatives burst out of my mouth and I am even
surprised at what I said.
I pray that those dust mounds will be aired and purified by the heaven's atmosphere and become
a sacred element of the air.
I pray that I will breathe in the same air as
His glorious strength to do only His will as
an answer to my prayers.

1Corinthians 15:51
Behold I show you a mystery;———But we shall all be changed—

A Prayer As A Poem—Richard A. Dixon

June 27

Fear Not - It Could Be A Blessing

On this day I pray that everyone will come
to that point in their lives to make
that ultimate commitment.
The fullness of life cannot be found until we
come to our senses to build
our spiritual confidence.
True faith some of the times does not really
come alive until we find our hearts filled
with pain and tears.
It is at this time that we search our soul and
hunt for the answers for our whole
being is filled with fears.
I pray that we can see that when we are hit with
a tragedy it could be a blessing that comes
in a spiritual disguise.
I pray that we can see that it is a wake up call
to revive our heart to be a blessing that
comes completely spiritualized.

Isaiah 57:15
For you say to the high and lofty———to revive the spirit of the humble spirit and to revive the heart of the contrite one.

A Prayer As A Poem — Richard A. Dixon

June 28

Showing Love To Do The Right Thing

I pray on this day O God that I will find
the wisdom to replace the right
way with only your love.
Sometimes God we are faced with the decision
to do the right thing but that might not
be the resolve to think of.
There may be a critical time when the world
and your mind tell you what is right
but God tells you to care.
Be kind with the love of God and His spirit,
when all else tells you different,
then you start with a prayer.
I pray that I will be able to discern that most
critical situation and not to think too much
how the world plays its part.
I pray that by doing His will and by receiving
His word will be the right way to transfer
His love from heart to heart.

1 Samuel 12:23
Moreover as for me———I will teach you the good and the right way—

A Prayer As A Poem—Richard A. Dixon

June 29

Forever In My Very Soul

On this day I pray to remind myself that
my God is with me always when I am
walking down the street.
He is there not only to guide me but to protect
me and He will keep me on that
track of being discrete.
Whether I am in a car with friends or by myself
I can feel His spiritual nudge that will turn
me in the right direction.
Whether I am in a crowd or one on one I find
my spirit interacting with my God's to
assure that glorious connection.
Talking and listening and being completely conscious of my God 24/7 gives me that enormous
feeling of heaven on earth.
My communion with him in any place makes that
place sacred, I am blessed and He makes me
care for all of its worth.

2 Corinthians 13:14
The grace of the Lord Jesus Christ, and the love of God, and the communion of the Holy Ghost, be with you———

A Prayer As A Poem — Richard A. Dixon

June 30

We Are Alive So Let's Live For Each Other

I pray on this day to enjoy that I woke
up to breathe the air as the
new day sunrise.
I pray and thank God for the talk that I had
with Him this morning and His grace
that I am alive.
I pray and give thanks that this day has given
me another chance to improve upon
my skill and drive.
This day has opened its doors again for me to
help others and to care for them in His way
for today I am alive.
Recognizing and being ever conscious of my God
giving me His grace and the power of His love
to help others to survive.
I pray that this day will open hearts to the chance
of living a better life so that we can
all say we are truly alive.

1 Thessalonians 4:15
For this we say unto you by the word of the Lord, that we which are alive and remain unto the coming of the Lord———

A Prayer As A Poem — Richard A. Dixon

July 1

The Good Things Happen Because You Are Blessed

I pray on this day that I will forever see
that glorious light that tells me
that I am blessed.
It is only through His saving grace that
I live and in me his gift
brings out the best.
Being fortunate and lucky is definitely not my
way to explain why I now walk by the
side of my LORD.
I know that He has always been with me and
not just because of my efforts that I
receive His award.
I pray now to show my humble thanks by walking
on His ground to get closer to Him and Heaven
and away from sin.
It is not luck and being fortunate, it is only His
blessing that will lead me to happiness that
comes from only Him.

Psalm 103:2
Bless the LORD my soul, and forget not all His benefits———

A Prayer As A Poem—Richard A. Dixon

July 2

Pray To See The Whole Picture

I pray on this day that we can visualize the
scenario that what God said that in dying
He restores our lives.
Although we as humans generally regard
death as a highly saddened event in
which our emotion thrives.
I pray that we can see the parallel as a plant
that dies and leaves a seed to transfer and
grow to blossom ripe.
When we die, God restores our souls and like
the seed our souls are revived so we become
His new prototype.
I pray that we can see the real picture and
accept God's plan and He blesses us until
the day we die.
I pray that we also see that in the hereafter His
plan for us is to be in heaven with Him
and to eternally fly.

Psalm 23:3
He restoreth my soul He leadeth me in the path of righteousness———

A Prayer As A Poem — Richard A. Dixon

July 3

Let God Save You Again And Again

I pray on this day for all that have lived for a while
in God's world but somehow they fell
back into the dark.
The temptations of this world influenced them
to take up selfishness and all of the things
that tear us apart.
I pray that they will not lose hope because of that
negative turn-a-bout which leads away
from the spiritual path.
I pray that they will reach down and seek that
strength from God to take them away from
that devil's wrath.
Our God has saved you before and will save you
again and again our Lord Jesus is forgiving, He
will never forsake you.
I pray that they will see that all they have to
do is to come to Him in forgiveness and
He will see them through.

Psalm 100:2
Serve the Lord with gladness, come before His presence———

A Prayer As A Poem — Richard A. Dixon

July 4

Let's Find That Independence From Sin

On this day I pray in commemorating our
Independence Day, to search and
find its ultimate meaning.
The key to all of this is the word freedom but
to find the real answer day, to search and
employ diligent screening.
We know that in this world we fight for human
rights, freedom of movement, our right
to write and right to speak.
To me, I think that if we would instill in ourselves
that spiritual balance that would
be the first to seek.
I pray that by putting first things first and let the
priority be receiving all of those spiritual things
that come directly from above.
I pray and I have found out that freedom from stress,
strife, and fears will lend serenity to solve
problems with God given love.

Roman 6:18
Being then made free from sin, you became the servants
of righteousness———

A Prayer As A Poem—Richard A. Dixon

July 5

For This Day God Is In My Heart

I pray on this day that my God the Father, the
Son, and the Holy Ghost will
reside in my soul.
I pray that for this twenty-four hours the divine
spark in my soul will lend energy to maintain
my spiritual control.
On this day I pray that all of my thoughts will be
from my soul so that my conscious
will be totally sin-free.
What comes from God and what comes within builds
my character and no one on earth will
take that away from me.
On this day I pray that when I speak to others may my
words be like the words that my
Lord Jesus would say.
May my actions be sensitive and reach out to all of
my fellowman and they will know that I am doing
His will this given day.
I pray that the strength that I receive from my God's
spirit today will be more than enough to
help complete His will.
I pray that my faith will remain strong today and I
will do His will even better each coming day and
for now and until.

1Peter 3:15
But sanctify the LORD God in your heart———

A Prayer As A Poem — Richard A. Dixon

July 6

Your Spirit Means The Most

On this day I pray to intensify the strength of my
spirit that holds the key to
my ultimate goal.
Your life is your opportunity to train that spirit
and to keep the flow for the goodness
as it is told.
I pray to keep a grip on life and to keep it in mind
from this moment exactly what my purpose
is on earth.
To live, to feel His freedom, to grow and evolve
in the spirit of the soul, seeking the LORD
for all of its worth.
I pray to in reality feel my forward movement getting
closer to my GOD in mind and spirit
every single day.
I pray that all will discipline themselves and hold
that determination so that everything will
be done His way.

2 Corinthians 3:17
Now the Lord is that spirit: and where the spirit
is———

A Prayer As A Poem — Richard A. Dixon

July 7

It Is Your Choice Only

I pray on this day and let us get it right,
that it is not God's will to send
anyone to hell.
This decision is totally your decision to
make, it is you that
rings that bell.
I pray to know that God will never send
anyone to occupy the realm of
Satan's space.
I pray to know that God honors your will not to
choose Him even though you chose that sinful
devil's place.
I pray that God bless and have mercy on them for they
know not what they do, now they are
lost souls and sinners.
I pray to fully understand that all of God's children
can use their will power to choose GOD
and become His winners.

Proverbs 27:20
Hell and destruction are never full: so the eyes of man
are never satisfied———

A Prayer As A Poem — Richard A. Dixon

July 8

GOD Help Us

I pray on this day GOD help us to help them
who are so far gone that they cannot
help themselves.
Give us all of the strength to reach out and
bring them up to you from their
lonely shelves.
I pray GOD you will allow us to show the lonely
and weak that we really care
and love them.
I pray that you will guide us in guiding them to help
them to release themselves from
their chronic problems.
I pray GOD that you will help us all by having us to
come together as one with that spirit to follow
only your sign.
Allow all of your lights within us to shine on each
other's hearts so that none of us will
be left behind.

Psalm 21:2
My help come[s]? from the LORD which made heaven
and———

A Prayer As A Poem — Richard A. Dixon

July 9

A Wonderful Story That Could Be Yours

I pray on this day and I think of the lives that had
troubles and found themselves with results that
were out of range.
They did not do too much praying and they
found out that they could not make one
significant positive change.
At some point and time they begin to pray and
they made that commitment to put
it all in His hands.
They begin to feel that satisfying relief, they once
felt they were drowning, now that
feeling is on God's land.
By coming to him in prayer we can climb that
ladder and our priorities change from the
treasures of the earth.
In prayer we can find that quiet satisfaction and
this is why I pray to receive from Him
my spiritual rebirth.

Chronicles 7:14
If any people————shall humble themselves and pray
and seek my face and turn from their wicked ways; then
will I hear from heaven, and will forgive their sin————

A Prayer As A Poem — Richard A. Dixon

July 10

Be Careful What You Put In Your Life

I pray on this day that I will be mindful in how I
meet and greet all in relationships that will
come my way.
I will approach each one with the responsibility to
be kind in my remarks and not be the one
to cause dismay.
I pray to be constructive rather than destructive and
to be open-minded when trying to turn that wrong
and make it right.
I pray that my spirituality in doing God's will find
the answer and will be the end result because
of my spiritual fight.
I pray that we will all think with our hearts in coming together in this world to find that common
ground to eliminate doubt.
I pray to keep the faith and remember the world's
saying and follow its meaning, "It is what
we put in is what we get out".

Philippians 4:6
Be careful for nothing; but in everything by prayer——
–Let your request be known unto God———

A Prayer As A Poem — Richard A. Dixon

July 11

Forgiving And Patience Go Hand And Glove

I pray on this day as I go through this life in
this world our Lord Jesus has been the
most forgiving of us all.
I pray and know that regardless of our ways in
failing to do His will He still answers our
plea when we call.
I pray and know you should understand there is
no compromising when it comes to
receiving your salvation.
It is written that it is through our Lord Savoir
Jesus Christ that we receive our
full affirmation.
I pray at times instead of action and countless words
to enlighten a heart you will find the Lord's
guidance of silence is best.
I pray to always know that it is patience that goes
hand in glove with forgiving that brings
the Almighty spiritual success.

Hebrews 12:1
Wherefore————Let us lay aside every weight and the
which does so easily beset us, and let us run the patience
of the race————

A Prayer As A Poem — Richard A. Dixon

July 12

I Am Only Selfish When It Comes To God

I pray on this day and may be rightfully called
selfish for it is in my determination to be with
my God the Almighty.
Let that selfishness be only that devotion to
serve Him and to do His will entirely
and not just slightly.
I pray that my devotion will be seen by all by the
way I walk and talk and let His light that shines
within me come into view.
I pray that that light will show others their way out of
their darkness so that they can find answers
that they never knew.
Let my divine blaze kindle all of those divine
sparks that which who are now barely lit
and they are almost smothered.
I pray that my devotion will become a flame that
will burn deep in my soul and warm the
hearts and souls of others.

Revelation 21:6
And He said unto me, it is done, I am the alpha and the omega, the beginning and the end———

A Prayer As A Poem — Richard A. Dixon

July 13

A Fulfilling Life

On this day I pray and thank God for
His goodness that placed
us on this earth.
I pray and I give thanks to God
for the gift that He
gives us at birth.
We daily pray and go through
all of our lives facing this
world's tribulation.
I pray not to be misled at those
times because of our world's
tempting jubilation.
I pray to be wise and resolve those times
when we wonder and have
doubts of who we are.
I pray to God to give me the strength to find
those answers whether
they are near or far.
We pray to know that everyone has that
special gift and we should
all find what is yours.
We should pray and fulfill that
purpose so that all of His
purpose will be assured.

Romans 8:28
We know that all things work together for them that love God,
to them who are called to his purpose.

A Prayer As A Poem — Richard A. Dixon

July 14

Walking And Talking As One For All

I pray that we all walk together as one
and I pray that we all talk
together as one.
I pray that we all listen to His word as one, yes,
coming together when all
is said and done.
I pray that when times are hard and we are
weak, I pray that He will carry us
until we are strong.
I pray then we will be able to walk with His
strength and we will walk in cadence with
Him where we belong.
I pray that we will all be still and hear what He has
to say for His word will indeed guide us to
what's in heaven above.
So let us all pray and open up our hearts for it is all for
one and one for all in His world of
good and world of love.

John 13:34
A NEW COMMANDMENT———THAT YOU LOVE
ONE ANOTHER AS I HAVE LOVED YOU———

A Prayer As A Poem — Richard A. Dixon

July 15

Just The Urge To Pray Is A Blessing

On this day I pray because I have been blessed,
I have taken this time as
quality time to pray.
The reason that I go through this spiritual com-
munion, I find a need to talk to my God
each and every day.
I thank my God, my creator has given me a way
to bond with Him, my God and my soul
form that lifeline.
I thank Him for giving me that will power to think
for my self and I choose His way and perception
of eternal time.
I pray to know that we are tested daily to show our
drive to keep His will and He cheerfully puts our
problems in His hands.
My prayer to God is heart to heart and it bonds our
spirits and it guides us to help others to better
this mixed-up land.

Numbers 6:21
The LORD bless you and keep you———

A Prayer As A Poem — Richard A. Dixon

July 16

The Greatest Of All Meetings

I pray on this day as all days to have my meeting
with my LORD so that He and I
can talk spiritually.
I pray that this spiritual happening will be as
all other communions, giving me
His strength freely.
We all must know that it is through these contacts
that we can consistently find
serenity and peace.
We should pray that these rendezvous with God
should be a must and that our visit is
on an eternal lease.
I pray that I shall forever meet with my God and
Savior Jesus on a daily schedule for its value
and ultimate satisfaction.
I pray that I will receive each time more in the meaning of life so that I can be a positive pacesetter
in all of my reactions.

John 4:24
GOD IS A SPIRIT: AND THEY THAT WORSHIP HIM
MUST WORSHIP HIM IN THE SPIRIT AND TRUTH.

A Prayer As A Poem — Richard A. Dixon

July 17

Place Your Heart And Soul In His Home

On this day I pray that I will try to help others to
bring their heart and souls and live in
the Almighty's home.
Our Father in heaven has enough room for all in
His house and will save us from
our prodigal roam.
I pray that we will put as much energy or more
to establish our residence and making
Heaven Number One.
At times I believe that we are more interested in
housing our bodies and leaving our souls
to live in none.
When we live outside His home you are not protected
from the wrath of sin and your heart never
warms up right.
I pray that by bringing our souls out of the cold and
sharing His grace we will have joy and
His spiritual might.

2Corinthians 5:1
———We have a building of God, a house not made with hands, eternal in the heavens———

John 14:2
In my Father's house there are many mansions———I go and prepare a place for you—

A Prayer As A Poem — Richard A. Dixon

July 18

On This Day I Pray

On This Day I Pray
I will always gladly walk by the side of my LORD.
On This Day I Pray
I will always talk with Him and be in accord.
On This Day I Pray
I will listen to Him and receive His spiritual rewards.
On This Day I Pray
When I think I am aware of His presence in my mind.
On This Day I Pray
When I speak let every word be from Him for mankind.
On This Day I Pray
When I do let Him guided me so to be well defined.
On This Day I Pray
To breathe in all that heaven gives.
On This Day I Pray
To share and care so that others may live.
On This Day I Pray
To show compassion so that I will forever forgive.
On This Day I Pray
To only use the love of God to do what I do.
On This Day I Pray
To reach out always to everyone so that we all can
be a part of His spiritual breakthrough.

1Thessalonians 5:17
Pray without ceasing———

A Prayer As A Poem—Richard A. Dixon

July 19

The Hand That Gives Life

I pray on this day that His hand will touch
my heart and soul as He
has done before.
I pray to feel the power of His spirit taking
control of my being to the deepest
part of its core.
Each day in my prayers to my God I can feel
the power of His hand that protects
me on my way.
It is because His touch has that strength to change
my weakness to courage so that I
can make my day.
He has taken special interest in the bond of mar-
riage for He has ordained the matrimony
of being man and wife.
I pray that it is only through Him that we can
receive His goodness and it all comes from
His touch, the hand of life.

Psalm 90:17
And let the beauty of the LORD our GOD be upon us:
and establish thou the work———

A Prayer As A Poem — Richard A. Dixon

July 20

Help To Spiritualize, Not Criticize

I pray on this day that I pray enough to keep me from
judging others negatively when
I know it is wrong.
I pray today to strengthen my compassion
to help others to get back in good
where they belong.
At these times when a person's heart is pleasing for
help we should forget ourselves and not
impose our preaching.
This is not the time to magnify the bad side, be
constructive, look for a positive resolve for
this act of breaching.
Bad mouthing has never been the solution to help someone
get back on their feet, give them
hope in being spiritually.
I pray that God will forever guide me and let me be that
hope for those who need it so they
can live peacefully.

Roman 8:24
Likewise the spirit also help————but the spirit itself makes intercession for us with groaning which cannot uttered————

A Prayer As A Poem — Richard A. Dixon

July 21

All That Is Well Ends Well

On this day I pray with a bit of a wondering thought
in my mind on why it took me so long
to get where I am.
There are many that say that they believe in God and
that they have a heart that follows
the spiritual program.
I pray and know now that before I gave myself com-
Pletely to my LORD depended many times only
on my energy and way.
Many times after my irrational decisions I found myself
reviewing my mistakes and I always ended up
having a bad day.
I pray that what I know now and if I knew it back
then I could have been walking by the side of my
LORD instead of being on His back.
I pray and know now that He carried me until He rid
my Heart of torment and He filled my soul with His
Spirit and put me firmly on His track.

Matthew 10:22
And you shall be hated of all men for my name sake; but
he that endured to the end———

A Prayer As A Poem — Richard A. Dixon

July 22

Man Created In God's Image

I pray on this day that I am heartily sorry
to have tarnished my being
that God created.
Because I was created in my God's image my being
was proclaimed as a temple for Him and
to be celebrated.
But somewhere along the way our will power misdi-
rected God's priorities and at times we were
influenced into sin.
I pray to know that my Lord Jesus Christ died for our
sins my task now is to ask for forgiveness
by coming to Him.
I pray daily and search my actions for now I am whole
and I will keep my heart open so
He can enter.
I will continue to strive to do His will forever and will
find no need to do wrong for God is
my eternal mentor.

Genesis 1:27
So GOD created man in His own image, in the image of GOD———

A Prayer As A Poem — Richard A. Dixon

July 23

Forgive, Forgive, And Forgive

I pray on this day to step back and take a complete
look at just how many times that I should forgive
according to our oath.
I know it is written in the Bible, the number is
seventy times seven or seventy times seventy
no matter GOD approves them both.
It is generally accepted in our world that three
strikes you are out and in this life the chances
do not pass that count.
I pray to commit to God's numbers for I know the
outcome will result in true spiritually and success
will be a paramount.
I pray that my heart and soul will forgive always as
God's way for from experience His way is the way,
I don't even think of a second guess.
In forgiving the response is always a trying fete
to fulfill but if we listen to God our
future will be better and blessed.

Ephesians 4:32
And you be kind one to another————forgiving one to another————

A Prayer As A Poem—Richard A. Dixon

July 24

The Desire Of Wanting To Be Saved

I pray on this day for those aching hearts
that are asking why can't they rid
themselves of sin.
I pray that they will find out that pleading thought
to change is a saving thought to stop
that sinful spin.
I pray that these persons will cross my path and I pray
that my LORD will guide me to guide them
right into His arms.
There is no earthly power that can bring peace and
put love in their heart and take them away
from future harm.
I pray that the lost ones will just admit that they can
not depend on themselves, they need God
to carry their load.
There is no greater satisfaction then receiving the spirit
of the LORD to face this world, and by
walking on His road.

Psalm 20:1 and 6
The LORD hear thee in the day of trouble——Now know
that the LORD save His anointed——

A Prayer As A Poem—Richard A. Dixon

July 25

Without My God There Is Nothing

I pray on this day and say if it was not for
my LORD that I will be wondering
just what to do.
If it was not for my Lord Jesus I would probably
be confiding only in my strength
to see me through.
I pray to face the reality and to thank God
for the creation of this universe made
only by His hands.
With the knowledge and the understanding my GOD
has given me I know that it was His wish that
He placed me on this land.
I pray to know that if there was no GOD in heaven
our earth would be in total sham and there will be
no one to hear my prayers.
I pray to know that if it wasn't for the love that
my LORD put in my heart I would be alone
with no one to care.

Proverbs 1:7
The fear of the LORD is the beginning of knowledge but fools despise wisdom———

A Prayer As A Poem — Richard A. Dixon

July 26

The Lesson Of Life Means The Most

On the day I pray that we will learn a lesson from
Jesus, who stuck to His plan that took
Him to the cross.
In His life He did not allow anything to deter Him, He
focused Himself to win His goal, there was no
thought of a loss.
Constant talks with the Almighty, receiving His strength
making Him your destination, determination should
be your guideline.
These standards have been proven by Jesus and being
our way to win over sin, He can make our light
glow with a spiritual shine.
With the strength and spirit of GOD, we can cross any
valley, climb any Mountain, our spiritual efforts
will not be diminished.
I pray that we will win and pass this test of life in
the games that the world plays and when we win
we can say, "It is finished".

2Timothy 4:7
I have fought a good fight, I have finished mycourse, I have kept the faith———

A Prayer As A Poem — Richard A. Dixon

July 27

The Power Of Faith, Prayer, And Trust

I pray on this day to capture and use all of the
power that faith empowers to give me
a defined direction.
We know that faith is the assurance that every-
thing will be all right because of
His spiritual connection.
Faith also empowers our prayers that strengthen
our faith, the more we pray the more trust we
can put to spiritual use.
Faith, prayer, and trust, working together give us a
power that can not be equal to anything that man
on this world can produce.
I pray that keeping the faith is not just an assu-
rance in believing, it's a path that leads
to living forever and ever.
I pray that bonding with God in faith, there
will be nothing that I should
fear never, never, never.

Psalm 33:21
For our heart shall rejoice in Him because we have trusted in His name———

A Prayer As A Poem — Richard A. Dixon

July 28

Your Comfort Zone Could Be A Hindrance

I pray on this day not to just do for myself
and not lending a hand to those
who are in need.
I pray that I will not just support me and neglect
my fellowman for when they are in trouble
this is where I should proceed.
I pray not to be controlled by excuses that will take
me away from any chance
to do God's will.
I pray to get up from my comfort seat and listen
to my LORD and climb
that steep hill.
I pray today and always not to wait for someone
to come and ask me for help, I pray
to take that lead.
I pray to know that it is in giving that we receive
His grace and in giving is the loving
way I can succeed.

Roman 12: 1
I beseech you therefore, brethren by the mercy of God that
you present your bodies in living sacrifice, holy———

A Prayer As A Poem — Richard A. Dixon

July 29

March On, March On

On this day I pray to march in step with
my God as we confront the
tribulation of our times.
I feel proud being in the regiment of the spirit
marching toward His heaven and
it's a glorious climb.
Marching for all to replace the evils of hate,
marching and assuring others that His
army is marching on.
I pray that all will join us in our victory
march, fighting sin until
it is all gone.
I pray to walk in His light spreading His word
letting everyone know that good is
our ultimate goal.
I pray that the numbers in our marching will
increase day to day until our efforts
will save all souls.

1John 1:7
But if we walk in the light, as He is in the light, we have fellowship with one another———

A Prayer As A Poem — Richard A. Dixon

July 30

Facing The Fearful Time

On this day I pray to remember as knowledge,
the fearful times that I experienced and pain
was my only friend.
I can recall calling out to my God to help me to
ease the pain, it looked like I had come
to a dark dead end.
It seems that all of us call on our God when
things get so hard they seem
impossible to bear.
I pray that we will all realize that when fear
enters our minds and to face the truth
gives you a scare.
I pray to be filled with His glory to prepare me
for future fearful times to assure my soul
will not feel lost or misplaced.
I pray that through these experiences we should
learn to talk to God on a daily schedule so that
we all can build on His grace.

Psalm 56:3
When times I am afraid, I will trust in THEE———

A Prayer As A Poem — Richard A. Dixon

July 31

The Unseen Is More Powerful

I pray on this day to bring my attention to the
reality of things that I cannot see for they are
the wonders of the LORD.
The wonders of His Spirit, although I have never
seen it, gives me strength to succeed and is
just one of His rewards.
Believing that there is a world after life on
earth is written in the Holy Bible and is
authenticated by His sacred word.
Having faith is the key in believing in God and my
daily communion with Him secured my life with
others as He the Divine third.
Love is in my heart to care for others, instead of
being in discord He has given me order,
my life is on an incline.
My one on one talking to my God has proven to me
that He can and will give me hope, He has
spiritualized my mind.

Hebrews 11:1
Now faith is the substance of things hope for, the evidence of things not seen———

A Prayer As A Poem — Richard A. Dixon

August 1

Pattern Your Life After God's Goodness

Let me pray on this day that we can find that
someone to look up to as a person who has
some spiritual might.
You would admire first the way the person talk
and what they talk about, you can find
sincerity in their fight.
I pray and delight at people who try to live their
lives with goodness in their hearts and they
seem to care for others.
Most of the time these are hard working average
people and during their day they pass their
spirit to one another.
Let us all pray to continue in His ways in help
ing others and it is good to frequent our
church as our spiritual tryst.
I pray that more would pattern after the word of
God right now and do not think earth,
think of being like Christ.

Acts 17:28
For in Him we live, and move, and have our
being———

A Prayer As A Poem — Richard A. Dixon

August 2

Spirituality Is The Way To Live

On this day I pray that I am blessed for I am
approaching life in all of its factions
in a spiritual way.
Having that foundation of being a Christian
I have a deep caring for all and that is the
substance of my résumé.
Spirituality goes beyond the world that we can
see, basically the power of the spirit originates
from powers unseen.
I pray to my God for He is the God of all
good of love and when we follow His
path, the bad is redeemed.
I pray to know that it is in fact that spiritual
force that brings us positive ends
gives hope to live forever.
I pray and thank God for my spirituality for
it does not discriminate, all nation
are on the sane level.

1 Corinthians 2:12
Now we have received, not the spirit of the world but the spirit which is of God———

A Prayer As A Poem — Richard A. Dixon

August 3

Your Divine Intention Would Be The Way

I pray on this day to think of a divine intent
and to grasp that divine intent and
use it for a guide.
I pray to be single-minded in my intentions so
that I will be in tune with God
to stay in stride.
You should be in the right frame of mind for
it is the key to put you
on the right course.
I pray no matter how complex things may get,
I pray to meet that challenge
with God's force.
Whenever, wherever you may be put your
intentions to work and let the purpose
be a divine way.
I pray that I will keep the spiritual thought in
action and with the Spirit, I will
do it without delay.

Hebrews 4:12
For the word of God is quick and powerful———
———and is a discerner of the thoughts and intents of the heart.

A Prayer As A Poem — Richard A. Dixon

August 4

To Be A Giver Is A Virtue

On this day I pray to see what I can give to
the world that would improve it and to
better it as being a giver.
I pray not to expect anything in return for
then my reasons would be selfish, over
these things I will not quiver.
To live to give may be a rare thought to more
than less, but in its true meaning this life
is a rewarding one.
You are truly blessed to possess this virtue for
our giving God praises these who
face real life head-on.
I pray today to take life on as a giver to take
that lead in reaching out to
those somehow fell.
I pray today that I will do better than ever
before to give as God would
and to do it well.

Acts 20:35
I have shown you all things———and to remember the words of the Lord Jesus, how He said, "It is more blessed to give than to receive".

A Prayer As A Poem—Richard A. Dixon

August 5

Being A Post Sentinel To Look out For God

On this day I pray to be a look out for all
of those chances where I can
share and care.
I will stay on my toes and not be blind-sided
by some evil force, I will start my
action with a prayer.
I pray with my look-out skills, I will be able
quickly to give hope to that someone who
has fallen into despair.
I pray that being a channel for my LORD will
bring joy to their hearts and will give them
peace with room to spare.
I pray to remain a sentry for my LORD for
those who may need a friendly word or a
hand to pull them out of a hole.
If we all will be a look-out for our fellowman we
could all become spiritual channel to
help save those lost souls.

Matthew 26:41
Watch and pray, that you enter not into temptation——

A Prayer As A Poem—Richard A. Dixon

August 6

Your Horizon Should Be The Heavens High

I pray on this day to raise my horizon of life up
to God and to focus on the things that are
in the heavens high.
I pray not to be caught in the things of the world
for there are too many gutters, there's
nothing there to glorify.
Sometimes our horizon does not get any higher
than ourselves and we can't see
anything but ourselves.
I pray that you will find out that your resources
to get things done runs out having everything
on a single shelf.
I pray that you will find that your horizon must
be higher than you can see to find
the spirit to lift you up.
As it is written that things on high open your heart
and you will be able to sup with Him
then with you He will sup.

Psalm 103:11
For as the heaven high above the earth, so great is His mercy———

A Prayer As A Poem — Richard A. Dixon

August 7

Turn Toward the Almighty

On this day I pray for those who say to themselves
that today they will turn over
a new leaf.
I know when these words are spoken the chances
of a change will most likely
not be completed.
There is only one way that a person can change,
he must put his life under His god's
control all lifelong.
He must cooperate with His God and admit
to Him and himself that his life is
going terrible wrong.
To be born again and to be spiritualized by God's
grace you will find your life as difference
as night and day.
I pray that all will turn their lives over to the Almighty God so that we all can rejoice as we
walk up His stairway.

Proverbs 3:5
Trust in the LORD with all thine heart, and lean not unto thine own understanding———

A Prayer As A Poem — Richard A. Dixon

August 8

Your Oscillating Mind Will be A bother

I pray on this day that I will have better control
of my mind that oscillates and responds in
an awkward way.
I believe our minds revert back to the past in
the form of an outburst and they try to put
things in disarray.
I pray not to harbor these thoughts in the least in
my mind, but my complaint is they jump up as
a unwelcome thought.
But I will not worry for I am striving for perfection and when I reach that goal I would rid of it
as in what I sought.
I pray in the meantime to make sure that I will
keep these unwanted thoughts to a minimal
so to cause no harm.
I pray to knock them out of my mind as quickly
as they appear replacing them with God's
spiritual glorious charm.

1 Corinthians 4:8
We are troubled on everyside, yet not distressed; we are perplexed, not in despair———

A Prayer As A Poem — Richard A. Dixon

August 9

Life Isn't Fair At Times

I pray on this day that I will not be that that
person when others will say,
"Shame, shame on you".
Your day stared out with plans to have a great day
but some reason things went wrong, you're
in a catch twenty two.
You made one mistake and your day sort of
went bad and for a while nothing or no one
made sense of it all.
It is then that you should find that private place to
be with your God to help you to calm yourself
so to ease your fall.
Pray to find that serenity with Him for when you
are at peace you can find answers that will
satisfy all that are involved.
I pray to know that life isn't fair at times, but God
is with me at all times and I will comfy in Him
for to make that resolve.

1 Peter 2:21
for even here————you called because Christ also suffered for us, leaving an example, that you shall follow His steps————

A Prayer As A Poem — Richard A. Dixon

August 10

To succeed Is Coupled With Doing

On this day I pray not to be that spiritual one
who will wonder whether I should I put
something good into action today.
There are times when we wait to do something
for no reason at all, like I will wait just
because it is time for a delay.
I pray to think that the more I do good the better things get and I may save a soul from
a world of uncertain fate.
To do less or nothing, I pray, is not the role that
I care to play for this may be
what failure dictates.
I pray consistently to be on the positive side of
the doing side because this, I believe, is the
part that God would play.
I pray that we all will proceed by being a doer
and that the positive ends will be the same as
the positive means today.
I pray that we will all see the joy in succeeding
that will result in those conclusions that could
be seen as a blessed array.

Galatians 6:9
And let us not be weary in the well-doing for in due season we shall reap———

A Prayer As A Poem — *Richard A. Dixon*

August 11

We Need That Powerful Divine

Let me pray on this day to keep the divine seed
that you have given me in
a growing mode.
May it continue to bear God's spiritual fruit
so enough will be available for
to walk His road.
His spiritual fruit carries the contents of honesty,
unselfishness, spiritual love for all
to partake in.
When you consume this God given gift, your
whole being becomes glorified building
to spiritual end.
I pray to God that we will all come to the master gardener to help cultivate our divine seed
to be forever prolific.
The sacred sent substance from this divine seed
will develop our souls and fill us
completely with His spirit.

2 Peter 1:3
According as the divine power has given unto us all things that pertaining to life———

A Prayer As A Poem — Richard A. Dixon

August 12

A World Of Many Worlds

On this day I pray to put my emphasis on the
fact that we live in the company
of many worlds.
To mention a few, there are the worlds of greed,
of hate, of sex, of lying, none implies
a Godly knurl.
I pray and will rely on my world of God of good,
of love, of honesty, to protect and not let the
bad inside of mine.
I pray that God will keep surrounding my
world with His spiritual shield so evil
will not be interbinded.
I pray to instantly to recognize these wicked worlds to
prevent their invasion with the help of
my God's spiritual aid.
I pray that I will not worry myself for I am assured
that it's all in His hands and I am
a member of His crusade.

1 John 2:15
Love not the world, neither the things that are in the world———

A Prayer As A Poem — Richard A. Dixon

August 13

Be Prepared For Your Daily Test

Let me pray on this day to remind myself that
our souls are tested to check the status of
our will power.
It is all part of our daily lives in making decisions
as a result to others actions, all times is
your testing hour.
God has this master plan that gives us the chance
to show Him that our hearts are open in
doing it His way.
We should all pray for His strength for in many
cases we take control and the results are
a dismal display.
I pray to my LORD to fill my soul completely
with His spirit so my will is subordinate and I
will be at my best.
I pray that all will allow God to execute his plan
and be His servant so we all will
pass His glories test.

2 Timothy 2:3
Thou therefore endure hardness as a good solider of Jesus Christ———

A Prayer As A Poem — Richard A. Dixon

August 14

Failure Is Not Apart Of The Plan

On this day I pray that to remember that
in this world, on all of us the
rain definite falls.
I pray that if for some reason that those chances
of some trouble may fall my way,
may I stand tall.
I pray to understand that the world will not
pass you by and not cause you some sort
of stress and pain.
If the laws of nature won't give you a kick some-
how an infraction of the moral law will bring
stress in your lane.
I will pray that when the wind blows trouble my
way and when its over that I will still be
in my spiritual space.
I pray and we should all pray that we run an
obstacle course and that it is best to be
with God and His grace.

Jude 1:25
Now unto Him that is able to keep you from falling, and to present you———before the presence of His glory———

A Prayer As A Poem — Richard A. Dixon

August 15

Working With God Is A Joy

I pray on this day that I will follow the reason-
able way to regard and spend my money
by being sensible.
I pray to take the spiritual approach by consulting
my God and also check some of the
words in the bible.
This may seem awkward to more than less that
that the things that we acquired through
Him have permanency.
When we go out to buy, we sometimes think
only lavishly, we buy what we see
not being practically,
It is important not to spend your money without
real meaning and do not be influenced
by the fancy ads.
I pray as all others should pray to seek the advice
from the LORD so that the goodness of the
value can be had.

1Timothy 6:7 and 10
For we brought nothing into this world, and it is certain that we can carry nothing————For the love of money is the root of all evil————

A Prayer As A Poem — Richard A. Dixon

August 16

Remember What It Means To Be On His Road

On this day I pray to remember all of the sacred
things by being on that one way road that leads
to heaven above.
On this road your walk get stronger, your talk
becomes more like His, your heart begins
to truly love.
On this road your knowledge increases and the
answers begin to come according to the time
you have travel.
You may had a time of adjusting to the terrain
during your first steps but soon you knew it
was smooth gravel.
I pray to know that my goal is to move at all time
to get closer to God every single
moment of the day.
I pray never to stop or turn around on the road for
this may offend my God, my will
is to do it His way.

Psalm 16:11
Thou will show me the path of life———

A Prayer As A Poem — Richard A. Dixon

August 17

I will Not Be Intimidated

I pray on this day that I will not be intimidated
by the forces of evils that come
close to me.
I pray and know that the strength that I receive
from my God will not be compromised
by any degree.
I pray that when the unwelcome demons come my
way they will give me a chance to pass
another spiritual test.
I live totally for my God and I want Him to know
that my whole soul, my life for Him is
my only interest.
I pray to know that my God and I are one and
that mean when you come for me you have
to come by God.
I am blessed and privilege to be in this position
that I am with Him for I am a true member
of His God squad.

Isaiah 40:8
The grass withers,———but the word of our God shall stand forever———

A Prayer As A Poem—Richard A. Dixon

August 18

Be firm In Your Spirituality To Achieve Goodness

I pray on this day not to take life lightly, showing
little interest of what even the
day may bring.
There are some people that are in their own
world that maybe they never heard a
church bell ring.
To care, to love one another, to share with them,
these are the things to assure
eternal for all.
Life on earth could be heaven on earth, but
focusing on world values, this is our
dismal downfall.
If we all would allow God in our hearts, this case
will be closed, and there will be nothing
more to discuss.
I pray to do what I can to influence others to see
that it is the spiritual life that instills the
goodness in all of us.

Psalm 18:2
The LORD is my rock——my God, my strength———

A Prayer As A Poem—Richard A. Dixon

August 19

Showing Kindness Is Good

I pray on this day to be apart of the under-
standing of people to people in showing
genuine kindness.
Being cordial and polite sometimes could be
the only way to come together without
being totally aimless.
I pray to know that our world has many diver-
sified customs and ways that I would
care not to pursue.
And I pray to know that it is generally
accepted when in Rome to do
as the Romans do.
I pray to know as long as the kindness is not
threatening any of God's laws, allow
all to be heard.
I pray that the person that that is receiving the
kindness maybe one day may help you to
pass on God's word.

Psalm 31:21
Blessed be the LORD: for He has shown me His marvelous kindness in a strong city———

A Prayer As A Poem — Richard A. Dixon

August 20

You could A Be Guiding Light

I pray on this day not just to entertain the
thought of being an instrument for God in
being a guiding light.
I pray that I am a true believer and the person
that I might meet today, to pass on to them
some spiritual insight.
I pray to think that the people that I talk to
feel better as a person after we have
had a joyful talk.
Because God is indeed always with me then
that person with me might also receive
grace as we walk.
Easing pain, giving someone hope could be
given to anyone with a kind word as a
channel for God through me.
I pray that the quality time that I spend with
others will be apart of God's plan to make
their hearts feel sinful free.

Romans 13:8
Own no man any thing, but to love one another———

A Prayer As A Poem — Richard A. Dixon

August 21

May My Last Day On Earth Be My Best

On this day I pray to live it with God's master
plan in mind and to put His complete spirit
in to all what I do.
My expectations is to have many more days in
which to live but there is no guaranty that I
will see this one through.
This is one reason that I will not take any chances
and be slack in my plan and always plan to do
better than yesterday.
It would be advisable for all to put their hearts in
everything that they do now, for tomorrow they
may be turned into clay.
I pray to capture every moment that this day can give
me and I pray that I can fulfill this day
in my positive conquest.
I pray to God that He will bless my efforts and will
find this day of all of my days that this one
is truly my best.

Job 8:7
Though thy beginning was small, yet thy latter end should greatly increase———

A Prayer As A Poem — Richard A. Dixon

August 22

Truly Love With Your Heart

I pray on this day to be sure that my heart and
my love come from my
God to share.
Genuine love that you pass on from heaven
is a force that can change you
to truly care.
I pray to maintain my spiritual flow that is apart
of God's main stream that supplies to
bind all of our souls.
The ability to pass God's love on to others must
be pure in heart even if it only someone that
you want to console.
Remember, it is important to not to be slight in
doing God's will you should be caring
to all concerned.
Pray not to be bother that you see no love for you
for if you follow God's rules, your true love
will be returned.

Ecclesiastes 8:5
Whoso keep the commandments shall feel no evil thing;
and a wise man heart discerns———

A Prayer As A Poem — Richard A. Dixon

August 23

You Should Never Feel Inferior Being In The Spirit

I pray on this day never let this world get me down
and make me feel that I can not
get things right.
I pray that my deep devotion to God's plan will
keep that flame in my heart and fill it
with His might.
We all have lows in our life where we do feel
weak, these are the times we should listen
for His voice.
I pray to hear His words, to understand His
plan so that I will make no mistakes in
completing His choice.
I pray always to secure my heart and soul with
His power so that I will never feel weaken
in my spiritual fight.
I pray to stand tall, to be firm in my determination to do His will, to walk steadily to
reach His heavenly height.

Isaiah 40:30
But the that wait upon the LORD shall renew their strength———they shall run and not be weary———

A Prayer As A Poem — Richard A. Dixon

August 24

Daily I Am Apart Of Him

On this day I pray that I will repeat my spiritual
routine as though they were second nature
in building my soul.
Each morning I will commune, meditate in
talking to my LORD to put me
under His complete control.
My ritual in making contact with people is to
respond to their actions by being sensitive to
their needs or stress and pain.
To be there for them, a kind word, a helping hand
as caring, to be a good listener, no matter
how much they complain.
Praying at the end of the day as in the morning, reading the Bible is the prime source in life to make
your heart sing hymns.
I pray that each day of my life that I will be available to do God's work as being what I do for
I am indeed apart of Him.

Matthew 28:20
Teaching them to observe all things———
I have commanded you and, lo, I am with you even to the end of the world———

A Prayer As A Poem — Richard A. Dixon

August 25

Pledging To Fulfill His Word

On this day I pray when I am confronted with a
task to do God's will, I will pledge to do
it with admiration.
My determination in making sure that I succeed
will be bargain with my life as
the stipulation.
To know the wonder of it all that this will be the
wish of my Almighty means more than what
this earth can give.
To honor His work in making my pledge would
be my spiritual chance to enhance my
life to eternal live.
I pray that I will always have my intentions in
order and that's what I am doing, it's not for
things of the world for me.
I pray never to seek personal fame or wealth, for
when I do God's work first my life is
rich in feeling joyfully.

Psalm 37:5
Commit thy way unto the LORD———

A Prayer As A Poem — Richard A. Dixon

August 26

At The Office At Work With My God

I pray on this day and look forward of getting
up and enjoying the idea of
going to work.
He assures everyone total freedom to think as
individuals but denies the existence of
sin to lurk.
Although I am on duty at all times, I still consider it an opportunity to be a channel
to do His will.
Whenever I finish doing His work, I feel good inside,
I know that I have helped eliminate
some evil frill.
My God, my boss, my guide, my friend, no one could
have been more blessed for these
spiritual conditions.
I pray until the end to be employed by Him and that
He will always call me to work on His
spiritual missions.

Psalm 107:8
Oh that men would praise the LORD for His goodness,
and for His wonderful work———

A Prayer As A Poem — Richard A. Dixon

August 27

Do What You Are Capable Of Doing

I pray on this day that I will always keep
in mind that I will continue to
strive for perfection.
I pray and know that this earthly goal may not
be fully reached but the striving
binds our connection.
God knows that I am striving to get closer to
Him so in the meantime I will do
the best I can.
I will not delay my challenging the world
because I am not perfect, I will not be
still and just stand.
I pray that all will not use this negative approach
of fear of making a mistake for God knows
we are not perfect.
I pray to depend on the strength of my God,
knowing that the **positive** ends will always
have a **spiritual** effect.

2Timothy 3:17
That the man of God be **perfect**———furnished into all
good work———

A Prayer As A Poem — Richard A. Dixon

August 28

Rethink Rebuild And Be Reborn

I pray on this day for all of those who has been
taken out of the world of good and now find
themselves in the dark.
I pray that on this day they will start rethinking
their status and get themselves back on
their spiritual mark.
I pray that in their thinking that they will not be
hesitance in their prayers, for somehow
your goal must be earned.
This decision along will initiate your rebuilding
process for He will forgive again and again
each time that you return.
I pray that they will never find themselves
aching, suffering with evil in
that devil's sinful hole.
I pray that they all will be reborn again with
God's grace in their being and
His spirit in their souls.

Psalm 51:10
Create in me a clean heart, O God, and renew a right spirit within me———

A Prayer As A Poem—Richard A. Dixon

August 29

Each Day Within Itself gives Me His Energy

On this day I pray because this day is here
and I have been given more spirit with
the new day of energy.
I pray that this power which originates in
heaven will be given to me each
as a request of urgency.
From day to day I am blessed because my zeal
and interest to do his will is intense as
or more than ever.
I am given this strength on a daily basis to
face the world and to work as a
channel and as a lever.
I pray to forever to be in His grace for the joy
can not be compared especially
in this world of sin.
I pray that I will always be overwhelmed by
His power to fight evil no
matter where or when.

Acts 1:8
But you shall receive the power after that the holy ghost
is come upon you———

A Prayer As A Poem — Richard A. Dixon

August 30

Not Under Your Control But God's Control

On this day I pray that I am truly living my
life in a state of serenity and
I strive to do good.
I pray not to be in that state of being
haunted by anxiety and
being misunderstood.
Some of us are under the impression that if
we walk right and talk right we are
as good as gold.
They have self-proclaimed themselves as the person
-who's-right, their real lives are
still out in the cold.
I pray that all will quiet that underlining
desperation with honesty by putting
God in their hearts first.
Your life under your control is not the way to go,
give that control to God to quench
that underlining thirst.

Psalm 27:11
Teach me thy way, O LORD, and lead me in a plain path———

A Prayer As A Poem — Richard A. Dixon

August 31

Joining My God In His Eternal Quest

I pray on this day to be alert and ready to
answer the call of my Almighty to
lend a helping hand.
I pray my awareness of His request will be vivid
in my mind so that I can successfully
fulfill His plan.
God has given me His grace and my soul
has been filled with His spirit
to pass it on.
My goal is to help and my burning desire
will not be still until His work
is completely done.
Walking by his side, listening to His word,
implementing His commandments is
the road to the eternal.
I could not ask for more for being apart of His
glorious pilgrimage as it is written
in His spiritual journal.

Psalm 34:3
O magnify the LORD with me and let us exalt His name together———

A Prayer As A Poem — Richard A. Dixon

September 1

Talk To Him In Prayer

On this day I pray to implement an honest
prayer to make direct contact to God,
who is everywhere.
I pray to be completely attentive in my talk
with Him giving and opening my heart
for Him to share.
I pray to Him for I have found that He will
each time give me some insight on what I
should do for that day.
In my prayer I can feel the energy and His
spirit flowing through my soul and my
stress is taken away.
I pray everyday to listen for His encouragement
that always gives me hope and a guideline to
do the spiritual thing.
He is the God of all that is good and in my prayers I conceive His grace and so again I say,
"He is King of kings".

Matthew 21:22
And all things, whatsoever you shall ask in prayer, believing you shall receive———

A Prayer As A Poem — Richard A. Dixon

September 2

Look at Yourself And See Who You Are

Let me pray on this day to look into the
mirror and take some serious time
to see who I am.
I pray to be honest with myself and look at my
character to see if my goodness is blocked
by an evil dam.
I pray to compare myself to what I was in the
past and to see if I have moved forward
or am I standing still?
God know that I must keep developing so that
I will do better than yesterday to
keep climbing that hill.
I pray to focus on moving forward for then
I will have little time to analyze for
that will be the key.
I pray to know that it is wiser to steady improve
and develop and to think what you are
becoming and will be.

Ephesians 4:15
But speaking in truth and love, may grow up into all things———

A Prayer As A Poem — Richard A. Dixon

September 3

Turn Your World Right Side Up

On this day I pray this time that people will
take a serious look at themselves to
see what end is up.
I pray that they will stop the anxiety of waiting
for the wrong things when God should
be filling their cup.
I pray that their honest analysis will give them
true answers of what they
have to confess.
If they can not admit to their wrongs they will
remain up side down and they
will steady digress.
I pray all to live their lives under the control
of God so that all their ups are up and
their downs are down.
Confusion will not exist on the way they came
or which way they go for their feet will
be on God's ground.

Romans 12:2
And be not conformed to this world: but be ye transformed by the renewing of the mind———

A Prayer As A Poem — Richard A. Dixon

September 4

Being Honest In All That You Do

I pray on this day to express in the meaning
just how important it is to put honesty
first in all that you do.
Honesty brings purity, pure in heart into the
picture, it is the foundation to real life,
this in God's overview.
I pray that my fellowman can see and avoid
the other side of the coin for it
lead to a big downfall.
Disguising the truth, being evasive are just a
couple of ways to a shady life and makes
life miserable for all.
I pray to build my life surrounded by truth so
that a strong chain of trust will be made and
true love will be our force.
I pray to know that God will be in our hearts and
we will care for each other and He will bless us,
this my God will enforce.

Philippians 4:8
Finally, brethren, whatsoever things are true, whatsoever things are honest————and if there be any praise, think of these things————

A Prayer As A Poem—Richard A. Dixon

September 5

Allow Your Mind To Be True At All Times

I pray on this day to realize that I must be good
in my thinking no matter where
I am or what I do.
Just because I might be secluded in some god-
forsaken place my thinking must
still be good and true.
God knows my every thought and everything
that I do so if for no other reason I will
be true to God above.
Some of the bad things that I may think when I
am alone, they may jump out of my mouth
and tarnish a true love.
I pray to know if you harbor bad things, they
become part of your being and you can not
control their action.
I pray to strive to clean my mind and to fill my
soul with only my God's goodness, so to avoid
any future infraction.

Proverbs 23:7
For as he think in his heart, so is he———

A Prayer As A Poem — Richard A. Dixon

September 6

Recommendations For A Better Life

Let me pray On this day and feel fortunate
that I can be of help to others because of
the life that I have live.
I thank my God that I have learned from my
mistakes and it has been proven it is not good
to be negative active.
You find yourself too many times ending up
making wrong decisions because you
thought you knew it all.
There was times that you would not accept others
advice because of your pride, you put
up a stubborn wall.
Then you find yourself without self-esteem, con-
fused in facing the world, then you found God,
He became your friend.
My life with Him has made me caring for all, I
have found peace, go to God for direction,
this is what I recommend.

John 11:35
I am the resurrection, and the life: he that believe in me
though he was dead, yet shall he live———

A Prayer As A Poem — Richard A. Dixon

September 7

Maintaining My Bond That Has Spiritually Sustain Me

I pray to take to heart and treasure those
intangible things that have given
me peace of mind.
I pray to sustain them and make them apart
of my being, right down from my
brain through my spine.
God has given me His spirit and has blessed me
and thanks God, no one can take
that away from me.
I pray to do all that is within my power to carry on
His work, to keep His spirit flowing,
to make us free.
I pray forever to strive to sustain what has been
given to me and to maintain my spiritual
bond with that force.
My life is now in His hands, He constantly gives
me direction and peace of mind, I'm blessed
to have no recourse.

John 8:51
Verily, verily I say unto you, if a man keep my saying, he shall never see death———

A Prayer As A Poem—Richard A. Dixon

September 8

There Is No Set Time To Pray

Let me pray on this day and understand that
there is a time for all things to perform
their purpose here on earth.
In my life it is a choice of time of prayer in
connecting with God, this virtue for me
to pray is a solid first.
In praying there is no set time to pray, you
allow your heart to be your guide and that
time is always prime.
Generally speaking, for individual praying is
primarily done when going to sleep and
religiously at mealtimes.
I find myself praying throughout the day for my
family, friends, neighbors, and peace so
we can live as one.
It is good to pray on a regular basis because you
will be assured of spiritual energy to fight sin
until its evil is gone.

Ecclesiastes 3:1
To everything there is a season and a time to every
purpose———

A Prayer As A Poem — Richard A. Dixon

September 9

Living With What God Has Given Me

On this day I pray that we will settle back and be
comfortable with the position that we
have in the community.
I pray that we will not find reasons to be
jealous of any of the neighbors it is
best to live in unity.
You may not have progress as much as your old
classmates, but remember that economics
is not everything.
There is no reason to be resentful for God has
given you a life with His spirit and joy and
peace that is like spring.
We should all live within our means and use
the things that God has given us to
keep goodness in sight.
I pray and thank God for my being honest,
and full of His love to do things His way
and to do them right.

Acts 17:28
For in Him we live, and move and have our being——We are also His offspring———

A Prayer As A Poem — Richard A. Dixon

September 10

Find God Now For It Is Not Too Late

On this day I pray for all whom are good and
is surly pure in heart to feel and keep that
spirit that controls their being.
I pray for all of those whom are lost in evil and can
find no good in that dark and they are terrified
of what they are seeing.
I pray if they will only find that fear in their
hearts of the lost of their God, for
their being now erode.
They will find a life of goodness for they only
need to admit their wrongs and they need
Him to carry their load.
I pray that somehow that all of the good in the
world can somehow connect with them to let
know that someone care.
I pray that that someone will get down on their
knees right now and let God hear their plea
in their earnest prayer.

Proverbs 8:35
For whoso find me find life, and shall obtain favor of the LORD———

A Prayer As A Poem — Richard A. Dixon

September 11

A War That Has Brought No Peace

Let me pray on this day and remember that ene-
mies that had no boundaries attacked us,
the purpose was to kill.
Along as they were marked Americans and all
that they destroyed were American owned,
their mission was fulfilled.
Everyone call this sort of thing war, this seems
to be the only way that nations attempt
to find answers to peace.
Somewhere along the way trust and love for all
get lost, hate, chaos, discontentment,
torment for all never cease.
I pray to God that we can succeed in peace, but in
spite of all we must continue to give thanks for
our blessing in every way.
We all should pray for an understanding for peace
with our enemies and pray that all souls
will join in one love starting today.

Matthew 24:7
For nation shall rise against nation, and kingdom against kingdom———

A Prayer As A Poem—Richard A. Dixon

September 12

Visualize The World As God

I pray on this day to visualize all of the world as
God will have it to be, filled
with goodness.
Visualize that God walks with you everyday to
guide you along your way, to help
you to progress.
Be conscious of your spirit that has been blessed
by His spirit to move you into the
purpose of the day.
Watch the sky and enjoy its wonders, sit and stare
and splendor at the flowers as
they seem to play.
I pray and behold all of the blessings that He has
bestowed upon me and the beam that shine that
shows me His road.
I pray, as we walk, for all to open their hearts and
survey what He has given you as you
take this glorious strode.

1John 1:3
That which we seen and heard declare we unto you——
——truly our fellowship is with the Father and the Son
Jesus Christ———

A Prayer As A Poem — Richard A. Dixon

September 13

A Day Of Joy And Confidence

On this day I pray with a confidence and joy
because I live beyond the stress
of the universe.
My connection with my creator have given
me a shield and I feel no earthly effects
of its evil curse.
Yes, God has given me that protection from
the evils of the world so that I can survive,
come what may.
He has place me in a sacred place where I can
find peace and be content with what may
come my way.
I pray that I can bring others into this place
where I reside so they can feel that
confidence and happiness.
God will gladly, with open arms, give you that
same protection for you to continue
your spiritual progress.

Psalm 91:2
I will say of the LORD, He is my refuse and my fortress:
My God, in Him I will trust———

A Prayer As A Poem — Richard A. Dixon

September 14

Get Rid Of That Boredom

I pray on this day not to find myself in a state
of boredom, thinking of myself and
feeling upset inside.
This emotional feeling is not good for thinking
or to be involved in something when
your mind is preoccupied.
I pray to know that God is the answer, He can
rid you of this emotional sickness and fill
you with real living.
By allowing Him to come into your soul, He can
show you how joyful it is to be alive
in caring and giving.
I pray that all others will find out and cross over
completely and be glorified by the
goodness of the LORD.
Their hearts, and souls will be so filled with His
glory, they would have forgotten about
the state of being bored.

James 1:23
For if any be a hearer and not a doer———

A Prayer As A Poem — Richard A. Dixon

September 15

Unify Your Mind For One Purpose

I pray on this day that I will maintain my
virtues, my religious standards, no matter
what occurs around me.
Sometime because of our frailties, we may
waver a little and things may not result
in being negative free.
On some occasions we might let our selfishness
become apart of what we are doing and take
things out of His hands.
We need to put up a prayer at this time and ask
for God's strength and not to do what in our
head but what's in His plan.
Pray before you act is always a helping and pre-
ventive way to assure that positive things will
be done by thinking with your heart.
Now, I pray completely at all times to think with
my heart for then I will be in unity
with Him in doing my part.

Ephesians 4:3
Endeavoring to keep the unity of the spirit in the bond of peace———

A Prayer As A Poem — Richard A. Dixon

September 16

Allow Your Heart To Tell Him All

Let me pray on this day that when I pray let me
know and understand where my heart is
for Him to hear my need.
Praying is a sacred within it and we must let
God know just how weak we are and
how much our hearts bleed.
As long as we are honest in what we ask God
will give us the energy and He will hear the
earnestness in our prayer.
As a true believer and your trust and faith in Him,
there will be no doubt that in His gift,
you will be the heir.
When we pray and let God know all of what you
feel and how you feel, this will empty our
heart of all of its pain.
Each time that I pray, I will bring it all to Him
and my soul will be free and I will be
that strong link in His chain.

1 John 1:9
if we confess our sins, he is faithful and just to forgive us our sins———

A Prayer As A Poem — Richard A. Dixon

September 17

Life Was Hard But Now It's Good

As I pray on this day, let us look at the things that
happened in our lives that had
an intricate reason.
Many have said to themselves that they went
through hell but now they can define
all of the seasons.
These experiences of aches and pain have made
productive people out of them and now they
have a sure role to play.
Their spiritual connection with God has shown
them their purpose and can see their reward
that comes on that final day.
Pray and do your work that you have been mode
to do God wants you to use your skill
until all good is done.
I pray to stay in my spiritual area to help better
this world and to enjoy this life until
I reach the eternal one.

Romans 8:28
And we know that all things work together for good——
who are the called according to his purpose—

A Prayer As A Poem — Richard A. Dixon

September 18

Do not be Daunted By Words from Others

I pray on this day not to be daunted by words
of others that may have a negative affect
on my feelings.
No matter how harsh the words maybe, the may
be some truth that brought about
this double-dealing.
Hearing negative things from others or hearing
what you care not to hear are unavoidable
in the circle you live.
We must learn to accept them and respond to them
positively and to learn from what
they may give.
I pray to look at these moments as a chance to find
answers that will better my life and avoid
of being a jerk.
I pray to have rid of that self in me so that my feelings will not be hurt and that I can move on
in doing God's work.

Matthew 12:37
For by thy words you shall be justified, and by thy words you shall be condemned———

A Prayer As A Poem — Richard A. Dixon

September 19

Winning And Losing In Life

On this day I pray to realize in this life we
go through the chances of winning or
losing everyday.
Factions of life is a two-sided coin you, succeed
or fail, it's pretty much up to you to
determine which way.
I pray that I will understand exactly what are the
things that gives me my life value and I will not
take them for granted.
I pray that I will never fail to lose them for I know
that it will be me that suffer the most and
I will be disenchanted.
I pray if by chance I do fail, may my heart become
wide open for Him to come in and
take away the fear.
I pray to win against this evil the next time
and to knock it out of my life, to
never again to reappear.

Matthew 16:25
For whosoever will save his life shall lose it:———Will
lose his life for my sake shall find it———

A Prayer As A Poem — Richard A. Dixon

September 20

Your Spirit Is You

I pray on this day that we all will face the
fact that it is what kind of a spirit that
we have is how we act.
It is how strong our spirit that points us in certain
direction and its quality will lead us and put
us on that spiritual tract.
I pray and know now why things went wrong in
my life before because I used my strength
to solve the problem.
I know now that I did not have my heart open
enough so God's spirit to enter so that
He could solve them.
To succeed in obtaining the good in life, we
need first that spirituality that is built by
His glorious hands.
I pray and boast and maintain this spirit that
God has given me for I am blessed to be on
His spiritual land.

Proverbs 16:19
Better to be of an humble spirit with the lowly———

A Prayer As A Poem — Richard A. Dixon

September 21

Allow God To Be Your Teacher

I pray on this day that I will not end up in the
wrong places seeking to unravel our spiritual
mysteries that seem rare.
Many angles of life are a mystery and many will
remain so, trying to find the answer would
be a questionnaire.
I pray to know that it is written that the fear of
God is the beginning of knowledge,
its aims are to save.
I pray and know that I have gotten much understanding and knowledge from God than
what the world gave.
There have been too many coincidences where people
have found God and miraculously became successful
in the world of the learned.
I thank God for His knowledge that I receive to live with
others and I will go to His sacred place
to receive it at every turn.

Psalm 119:99
I have more understanding than all of my teachers: for thy testimonies are my meditation———

A Prayer As A Poem — Richard A. Dixon

September 22

Today Let Us Pray For Good Together

On this day I pray and will seek out the way
that I should follow to make
a situation better.
I pray that I will remind myself to be compassion
and complete my day by forgiving
my debtors.
I pray to know that we must have a clear and a
free heart in working for the
positives for all.
Coming together as sisters and brothers as our
heavenly Father look on us as our
names are called.
Praying to make that something right and receiving
His directions and tract to follow so that we
all will be winners.
Let us all pray to improve our lives so the door
will be open to goodness so that all
of us can enter.

2Corinthians 6:2
———behold now is the accepted time; behold, now is the day of salvation———

A Prayer As A Poem—Richard A. Dixon

September 23

What God Thinks Of us Is All That Counts

I pray on this day to put in proper perspective
just what is my worth in this world that
is class-minded.
I pray that I will never fall into that same thinking of our decision-makers of
being color-blinded.
As a believer, a Christian, I hold myself high in
the eyes of my LORD and the meaning of
the cross on Calvary.
For God so love the world that He sacrificed His
Son to die for our sins and to give us
a way to eternity.
Everyone and that's everyone should look at themselves as God does, we should allow Him to
live in all of our hearts.
We will all then see through our prayers that we
are all His children and that we are all
branded with His trademark.

Romans 8:16
The spirit itself bears witness with our spirit, that we are the children of God———

A Prayer As A Poem — Richard A. Dixon

September 24

Let God's Kingdom Give us The Energy To Live In This World

Let me pray on this day to make sure that it be
known that this world is not the plan for
my eternal home.
This world changes from time to time, physically,
in attitudes and it changes have become
a shifting syndrome.
I pray now since I live in this oscillating world
that I will look forward in living with
God in His beyond.
To live in a kingdom that is characterized by being
stable in goodness, everything created
by His spiritual Wand.
I pray that this permanent home of God will be
home for all one day and that we all will live
forever in His grace.
Although things might be a little less stable in our
lives now, let's fill our hearts with God and think
of His ultimate place.

2 Timothy 1:7
For God has not given us the spirit of fear; but of power and love———

A Prayer As A Poem — Richard A. Dixon

September 25

We Should Feel As God Feel About who We Are

I pray on this day as we go through our time
in life that we are reminded that we
are not perfect.
It's not surprising to some that they will not go
through a day without error and lose some
kind of respect.
Our human physical body is complex and is
effective in surviving, but it gets more
vulnerable when it gets old.
As advanced as our technology has come, we
still fail in some areas, we still can't
eliminate the common cold.
I pray and thank God for being my creator
because to Him we are His most value
creation made by far.
God always shows us how he loves us by being His
children, I pray that we will feel that joy as
who we really are.

Romans 8:17
And if children, then heir; heir of God, and joint heir with Christ; if so———that we may be also glorfied together———

A Prayer As A Poem — Richard A. Dixon

September 26

Seek The Comforting Rest

On this day I pray that I continue to find
myself in the state of mind of peace
because of His gift.
By praying, communing with my God, my being
will be at rest and my spirit will
gives me that uplift.
We can go through life and go to sleep at normal
hours and receive that normal time
to get our rest.
But deep down inside of us our spirit has found no
comfort and our world is churning
inside at best.
We must pray and be aware of His presence in our
hearts and that we must completely make
His will our way.
Then we will feel that comforting rest deep in our souls
and serenity will cover our entire being
now and everyday.

Psalm 37:7
Rest in the LORD and wait patiently———

A Prayer As A Poem — Richard A. Dixon

September 27

I Will Not Compromise In Doing His Will

Let me pray today and let everyone know
that I will not compromise in my efforts
in doing His will.
I have been in those situations where I tried to
do things my way, I know now my way
was a foolish thrill.
Now I have God to take care of my life and I am
diligently aware of His presence and the
decision that He makes.
I pray never to delay in yielding to His voice in
my heart that tells me what to do, this is
the road I will take.
I pray through my spiritual knowledge, my deep
consciousness of His spirit in my spirit, I pray
He will control my mind.
I pray that I will not compromise in any way
and make sure His will prevail and I will
do this time after time.

Proverbs 28:20
A faithful man shall abound with blessing———

A Prayer As A Poem — Richard A. Dixon

September 28

A Journey And A Destination

I pray on this day because it is one more day
that I travel closer to my God and all
of His glory.
Reaching that destination to some have given them
fear but there will be more joy there if
we can foresee.
To the real Christian, reaching the heavens give them
drive to move forward and that His spirit will
fill their cups.
Then there is some that put too much emphasis on the
the journey itself, rather then the place they will
finally end up.
I pray to see God's heaven that has been reserved
for all of us to live in peace and goodness
for all times.
I imagine it in my soul each time that I pray to
God, it is the best vision that I have ever had
in my mind.

2Timothy 4:18
And the LORD shall deliver me———and will preserve
me unto His heavenly kingdom———

A Prayer As A Poem — Richard A. Dixon

September 29

When I Have done More Then Allow Me To Do Even More

On this day I pray that when I have completed
my work and then I did more, then let me
do even more.
I pray and feel so privilege to work with my God
and each chance I would like to register
a productive score.
They is no greater satisfaction than living this
life with God and the enthusiasm that I get
from His power.
Each time that I am doing things for Him my heart
is filled with joy and my hopes are as high as
the highest tower.
I pray and welcome every opportunity to do what
I can with God and whenever I can
because I believe.
I pray that my efforts will be an unending chain of
doings for Him, for when I do this, it is me
that also receive.

Galatians 6:9
And let us not be weary in well-doing———

A Prayer As A Poem — *Richard A. Dixon*

September 30

Quickly Ask For his Power

Let me pray on this day that if I feel even in
the slightest in doubting of my faith
in my LORD.
I pray to go to Him and ask Him to remove that
negative for it is not in tune with
His spiritual chord.
I pray that He will do what is necessary to put
my thoughts on an even-knell to do
His sacred work.
I pray that He will quickly refill my spirit with
His spirit, for without it things
could go berserk.
I pray that all will remember that we need to
be empowered by His power to maintain
that strong trust.
We need to keep our guard up to avoid this breakdown, the answer could be is to pray more often
for all of us.

1 Timothy 2:8
———men pray everywhere, lifting up holy hands, without wrath or doubting———

A Prayer As A Poem — Richard A. Dixon

October 1

It Is Not The Quantity But The Quality Of What You Do

On this day I will pray that I will put all of
the goodness that is in my spirit in
all of the things that I do.
My heart tells me that the good from your being
will give it value of purity
and to be eternally true.
We could spin a lifetime of spinning our wheels
and going around in circles giving us
goals of the pits of the night.
It's best to be that person because of your sincerity,
having bond with God so everyone
gets more to live gloriously right.
I pray from this moment on that I will not just
go through life just doing, I will make sure
that there is substance.
I pray that what I do will give people hope
and direction and then may they in return help
others with spiritual exuberance.

1Thessalonians 5:15
See that none render evil for evil unto any man, but ever follow that which is good———

A Prayer As A Poem — Richard A. Dixon

October 2

Insight, Hindsight, And Foresight

I pray on this day that God will give me that
insight, hindsight, and foresight to better
my way to forever live.
I pray that I will receive the understanding
from Him to see the real knowledge in all
that this world has to give.
I pray that my hindsight will let me filter out
the things that I should not use and use the
things for all to be insured.
I pray for God's foresight to see the handwriting
on the wall so that I will avoid evil
and make my life secured.
I pray that I will be able to utilize all of these
virtues and to work with God
to achieve what is good.
Being able to see the unseen with these God-given
tools, I pray that the results of all
will be fully understood.

Acts 2:25
————I foresee the LORD always before my face, for He is on my right hand————

A Prayer As A Poem — Richard A. Dixon

October 3

Thank God For Not Having Me Live In The Past

I pray on this day with the wonderful thought
that I have made a definite decision
that has brought me peace.
I know that I must continue to be consistent
in my behavior to insure that my
knowledge will increase.
I pray and acknowledge that my new life was
given to me by my Creator and I forever
want to be with Him.
My foundation of my life now is that His spirit
controls my spirit and to follow His way right
up to the top of the rim.
I am now blessed each day and I am living a
glorious life and it is the opposite of what
it had been.
I pray and thank my LORD that He has rid
me of that old life and it's a sure thing
to never see it again.

Ephesians 5:20
Giving thanks always for all things unto God———in the name of our Lord Jesus Christ———

A Prayer As A Poem — Richard A. Dixon

October 4

His Light Is The Same Day And Night

I pray on this day as I am reminded again
by the sunrise that this day began
with the brightness of the day.
I am also reminded by the presence of my LORD
that his light will always shine
on me as I go on my way.
I pray all will understand that although the night
comes, he will provide us His
light to carry on.
As it is written, the light of the day and night are
given to us in the same, the same
from dawn to dawn.
I pray to see that God is with us at all times
and the darkness carries no difference
when it comes to His grace.
Though we might not see as well in the darkness,
God will be our light and keep us
safely in His spiritual space.

Psalm 139:12
Yea, the darkness hide not from thee; but the night shine as the day———

A Prayer As A Poem — Richard A. Dixon

October 5

The Staying Power Of Your Faith

I pray on this day that the power of my
faith will be as strong today or
stronger than yesterday.
I pray that through my prayers I will
maintain that connection within
that honesty that I pray.
We should pray not to have our faith moving
in and out with God for consistency is
within its meaning.
We should pray to be steadfast at all times for
the more we are the more and greater the
power of our redeeming.
The strength of our faith will carry us through
the worst of storms, no matter how hard
the winds may have blown.
I pray that my faith will be so powerful that
I can pass some of its energy onto others
to strengthen their own.

John 15:7
If you abide in me and my word————you shall ask what you will and it shall be done unto you————

A Prayer As A Poem—Richard A. Dixon

October 6

This Wonderful Feeling Only Comes From My LORD

Yes my God, let me pray today and let my
thoughts of you fill my very soul and
ignite the flames of joy in my heart.
I pray and welcome that glorious feeling that
I know that your heart and my
heart are one spiritual part.
His heart and my heart working as one is the
most wonderful encounter that will
bring love to friend or foe.
The excitement of it all brings teardrops to
my eyes that come directly from heaven
and my whole being glows.
I pray to my God for all of the opportunities
to work with Him, to do things His way,
that He is my lighting rod.
I pray that all would open their hearts and
experience heaven on earth for all of
this goodness comes from GOD.

John 15:11
THESE THINGS HAVE I SPOKEN UNTO YOU THAT MY JOY MIGHT REMAIN IN YOU AND THAT YOUR JOY MIGHT BE FULL———

A Prayer As A Poem — Richard A. Dixon

October 7

When All Is Said And Done, His Will Is Right For Me

On this day I pray that I will continue to
do as I have done before and trust that
God's will for me is right for me.
I pray that I will be calm in my actions although
negatives may be falling my way,
more than there should be.
I pray that I will not be bothered by the
outcome of what has happened for this
will be His will for me today.
God knows all and sees all and he is telling
me that the positive end will not come
now, there will be a testing delay.
I will quickly ask him for His understanding
and for Him to guide me until this cycle has
ran its course, for things will be alright.
With my faith I know my day will come to know
that he was right in doing what he did for
me for our hearts will forever unite.

Psalm 19:8
The statues of the LORD is right——the commandment
of the LORD is pure———

A Prayer As A Poem — Richard A. Dixon

October 8

All Will Become Winners On That Day

Let me pray on this day and look forward
to that day when all believers will
be selected and called.
To all who found themselves on earth a bit
off-key with their peers will be
leaders in heaven's hall.
To those who were poor and found themselves
at the bottom of the list will enjoy with others
on high of being on top of the pole.
This will indeed be a day for those who were
without recognition on earth for they will
be in the spotlight and their story told.
All of the sinners that became believers will
become winners and those who were without
family will be heir to God's family.
I pray and thank God for that day will bring
to all an equality as brothers and sisters
with our heavenly Father for eternally.

John 6:40
And this is the will of Him———that everyone which sees the Son, ———may have everlasting life———

A Prayer As A Poem — Richard A. Dixon

October 9

Look And See What Your Soul Meant You To Be

On this day I pray to search my soul and
to look at what my feelings are
and why do I care.
The first things that I feel in my soul is that
goodness and love for all and I feel
my God put it there.
God is the creator of goodness and his will
has been placed in our soul as a divine
spark for us to use, as we will.
Through my life I have found that evil brings
nothing but evil, and good brings good
when His way is fulfilled.
I pray and ask why would we want to go against
what is instilled in our souls that will give
us a life for what it was meant.
I pray that everyone will kindle His spark
and become divine and live life to its
fullest spiritual intent.

Romans 12:2
And be not conformed to this world but be you transformed by the renewing of the mind, that you may prove what is that good———

A Prayer As A Poem — *Richard A. Dixon*

October 10

He Is Listening To Us And We Should Be Listening To Him

I pray on this day there will be times that I
may not be alert enough that God has
listened to my prayer.
Because of our human limitations we sometimes
cannot see the obvious and so we
do not become aware.
Time passes and we still wonder if God hears
our plea although the prayer has
already been answered.
We will see its fulfilling that came through the
most unlikely person and we welcome
its glorious transfer.
We must pray and know that God is there and
when we call with your prayer, He will
without a doubt respond.
I pray that our faith will be strong and that
our final prayer will be answered when we
meet in that blessed beyond.

Psalm 66:16
Come and hear, all you that fear God———

A Prayer As A Poem — Richard A. Dixon

October 11

Receive Your Spirit From God And Prepare To Share It

I pray on this day that I will receive my daily
spirit from my LORD to insure me that
I have enough to share.
If I am living right, I would have given away
some of my spirit yesterday to others
if it was only in a prayer.
Each day we must move closer to him so that
He can gladly refill our spirit so that
we will be prepared to give.
It is our God given privilege to pass it on
to others so that no one will be left
behind and all will be active.
I pray that the spirit that I pass on today
will be the same that flows through
others to strengthen our bond.
I pray that God's spirit will continue all across
the land for it is known that God's plan is
perfect for all who respond.

Psalm 51:19
Create in me a clean heart, O God, and renew a right spirit within me———

A Prayer As A Poem — Richard A. Dixon

October 12

Being Attacked By The Worst And Being Protected By The Best

I pray on this day to understand that I will
have to live my life every
single day until I die.
I know that I will have my share of pain
of torment, I will have good
days and a time to cry.
I pray and know that I will pull through it
all for I have my God to pull me
through, in this I will depend.
My LORD and I are well bonded and I know
that He will save me from total damage
and he will make my mends.
I pray and live with this assurance because
I have seen His power, He always protects
the ones who comes to Him and pray.
I pray and know that he will guide me with His
grace and spirit and that I need not fear
for my life will be glorified everyday.

Ephesians 6:17
And take the helmet of salvation, and the sword of the spirit, which is the word of God———

A Prayer As A Poem — Richard A. Dixon

October 13

I Humbly Thank God Again

Let me pray on this day to again be concerned
about being humble to my LORD
for all He has done for me.
I pray that I will remember to do this on
a daily schedule so that I will not be
remiss in what I agree.
The concerning thing about being humble is
balancing your self respect with the tolerance
of things that you know are wrong.
God delights with those who have patience with
the frailties of others for they gain self-respect
and their character becomes strong.
Being humble is a way that God would have us
to live, it allows the spirit to flow because
of the compassion that is used.
I pray that we all become a part of this gesture
and become humble for this is a gift from
God that no one should refuse.

1 Peter 5:6
Humble yourselves, therefore under the mighty hand of God, that He may exalt you———

A Prayer As A Poem — Richard A. Dixon

October 14

No Matter How Small The Deed Do It With All Of Your Heart

On this day I pray that I will accept life as
my LORD gives it to me for some days
are better than some.
I pray to know to appreciate the little things
in life for they may be the things that
will help me to overcome.
Although this day may not be one of my best
days, I will still search for the value
that this day may hold.
I know God will remain in my heart to guide
me in doing the small things, to have
His will to unfold.
To do the things that God wants me to do is
in my prayer today and I thank Him
for giving me this chance.
I pray that others will see the spiritual importance
to face all that comes our way and
to take that spiritual stance.

Colossians 3:17
And whatsoever you do in word or deed, do all in the name of the Lord Jesus, giving thanks to God———

A Prayer As A Poem — Richard A. Dixon

October 15

Leave Your Complaints To Him

I pray on this day not to complain about this
and that for this is not the way of my
God to a positive end.
Things that do not set well with you give them to
God for guidance and your act should
be more like a friend.
Again, pray and put those troublesome things in
the hands of God so that you can completely
put them out of your mind.
By doing this, we free our hearts to perform His
next command and we can be assured
the results will be in kind.
Let us all pray and remember as always that God
is in our presence at all times to protect us
from the work of the Devil.
As always, I will pray to keep the faith and
trust in Him so that I will always
be on His sacred level.

Psalm 27:5
For in the time of trouble he shall hide me in His pavilion–
———He shall set me on a rock———

A Prayer As A Poem—Richard A. Dixon

October 16

God's Force Can Counteract That Evil

Let me pray on this day that I will never feel
alone because things happen to
me and I feel some despair.
Life sometimes comes at us with such a force that
it gives us that thought that this
world is indeed not fair.
I pray that I will find safety in God for He is
the only force that can counteract that
evil force and turn things around.
I will not panic, I will remain in His spirit and I
will talk with Him and take a walk with
Him on His sacred grounds.
I pray my meeting with Him will give me the
eternal tools so that I can pull myself
out with His spiritual rope.
I pray that through my communion with Him
he will rid me of my pain and I
will see that eternal Hope.

Romans 12:21
Be not overcome of evil, but overcome evil with good———

A Prayer As A Poem — Richard A. Dixon

October 17

To Spiritually Love And Be Loved

On this day I pray again to continue to feel
that love that my LORD gives so
that I can receive its benefits.
I pray to know how meaningful it is to give
love earnestly and to share that love
to forever bond our spirits.
Genuine spiritual love that originated with
God initiates life within itself and
it makes you feel truly alive.
Be not concerned to think so much of being
loved but to be sure that your love is
in place so all can survive.
Spiritual love is that powerful force that can
indeed move mountains and can make life
better on earth for everyone.
I pray always to be a part of that spiritual force
to bring real life and happiness
where there once was none.

John 15:12
THIS IS MY COMMANDMENT, THAT YE LOVE ONE
ANOTHER, AS I HAVE LOVE YOU———

A Prayer As A Poem—Richard A. Dixon

October 18

His Sacred Master Plan Is Perfect For Us

Let me pray on this day to live life as my LORD
will have me to live.
Let me live that life to better help others in
the way that I give.
I pray that my God will put in his hands my problems
so they surely become a part of His plan.
Let my hands be the hands that reach out for others
hands to help them walk this land.
Let us all come to God and live in His world
so his spirit will flow from
one to another.
Let us all fight evil by bonding as one family
and make heaven on earth for our
sisters and brothers.

John 14:6
Jesus said unto him, "I AM THE WAY THE TRUTH AND THE LIFE; NO MAN COMETH UNTO THE FATHER, BUT BY ME".

A Prayer As A Poem — Richard A. Dixon

October 19

To Be There For All Who Are Near To Me

On this day I pray to be there for my family,
friends, neighbors, and all that I
make contact with.
Although this may be just another day to
some, I pray that my efforts today
will not be a myth.
I pray that I will not take anything for granted
and that I will let everyone know
that I care for them.
I pray that I will be there if my family or
friends need a helping hand, I pray
to help with their problem.
It may be just another day but it might be
that day when that someone might
need me the most.
I pray to be there for all who are near to me
or whether the places may take me
from coast to coast.

Corinthians 1:4
Who comfort us in all our tribulation, that we may be able to comfort them which are in any trouble———

A Prayer As A Poem — Richard A. Dixon

October 20

His Goodness Fills The Rome With Peace, Assurance, And Love

I pray on this day to make sure that my
atmosphere will be filled with the
goodness of His peace.
I pray to know that I will be able to live in
His spirit and because of His calmness
that will increase.
It is in these ideal circumstances that I
will be able to perform and succeed in
completing His spiritual mission.
When you are receiving a life of goodness
from the Almighty God, evil could never
survive under any conditions.
I pray to stay in the goodness of His world so
that I will be protected by
the power of His shield.
I pray to pass this goodness onto others so
that they will be better prepared
to do God's will.

Psalm 91:1
He that dwell in the secret place of the high shall abide under the shadow of the Almighty———

A Prayer As A Poem — Richard A. Dixon

October 21

Be True To Yourself And Rely On God

Let me pray on this day that I will look deep
inside of myself with a determination
to listen for God's voice.
My purpose is to make sure that I turn away
from myself and seek His word, for
his word for me will be my choice.
If I really want to achieve success and find
that real spiritual life I need to depend
on God's power.
I pray to be God's channel and be active
to help others achieve to be that
person of the hour.
I pray to know that as a person we sometimes
have bad thoughts and think wrong and
depend on ourselves to do.
We should be true to ourselves and know our
strength is futile, we should give it all to
God to see things through.

Psalms 12:6
The word of the LORD are pure words———

A Prayer As A Poem — Richard A. Dixon

October 22

There Are Strong And Weak Links That Bond Us With God

I pray on this day to realize that I am a
link in the chain that bonds us all
with God and His will.
I pray that I will be that link strong in my
faith that will be powerful enough to lift
us up that mighty hill.
It is how strong or how weak our individual
link may be that determines the
strength of the entire chain.
I pray not to be that one that causes failure
for someone or myself that will result
in torment or pain.
I pray that we all will strengthen our link in
the chain of goodness today so that its
power will withstand all.
I pray that others will bind with that chain
and make it even stronger so that no
one will ever fall.

Matthew 16:19
AND I WILL GIVE UNTO THEE THE KEYS OF THE KINGDOM OF HEAVEN: AND WHATSOEVER THOU SHALL BIND ON EARTH SHALL BE BOUND IN HEAVEN———

A Prayer As A Poem — Richard A. Dixon

October 23

My Spirit To Spirit Talk With My LORD

On this day I pray and find the need to introspect
and to reflect in my soul and
to validate just who I am.
In some deep thinking, it happens when you need
some answers about your intention
of a planned program.
In my meditations, I talk to my God and He
gives me strength to continue to
be what I have become.
He assures me that I am striving to get closer
to Him and he occasionally lets me
know where I came from.
I pray that each time that I meditate with my
God that He will give me more
grace so I can do more.
I pray that my soul to soul talk with my LORD
will give me direction and make me
one of His ambassadors.

1Timothy 4:15
Meditate upon these things, give yourself wholly to them;
that thy profiting may appear to all———

A Prayer As A Poem—Richard A. Dixon

October 24

There Is No Problem In Failure - He Will Help You Again

Let me pray on this day and bring it to the
attention that no matter how much you
fail, He will help you.
When you find that no one else will reach out to
lend you a hand, come to God and He
will see you through.
There are some things that you cannot pass
on and that you must bring your burden
to him yourself.
Pray, get down on your knees, and let Him hear
your heart and let Him know what is on
your troubled shelf.
Going in and out of the chances of life, we
know not what the day may bring, we
aim to follow His master plan.
I pray as a believer that I will always pray to
my Almighty and my first move is to put
it all in his hands.

Isaiah 55:7
Let the wicked forsake his way————and let him return
unto the LORD, and He will have mercy on him————

A Prayer As A Poem — Richard A. Dixon

October 25

The Heart Must Be Open For The Meeting Of The Minds

I pray on this day that we must be in synch
with the LORD to be cognizant of
all of His grace.
We lag behind in what God is doing for us
for our hearts might not be quite there
in His spirit-place.
The cooperation of our will power in conjunction
with how much we can perceive depends
on our communion and prayers.
Being pure in heart, being honest with yourself
and God's will influences your progress
and how much you will be aware.
I pray that my heart will be wide open to God
so that He can come in and fill it only with
His spirit so I can know all of His words.
I pray to understand all that He tells me and
that He will be where I am with others as
the loving and caring divine third.

Romans 12:16
Be of the same mind one to another———

A Prayer As A Poem — Richard A. Dixon

October 26

Being Conscious Of God Is A Spiritual Treasure

Let my pray on this day for the people who
have found the way to become conscious
of their God, their Creator.
It is indeed a spiritual connection that co-start
with that inborn spark of wanting to do
right now and forever more.
Somewhere in our lives we came to a definite
conclusion that the force of good gives us
a better life to proceed.
We found out that our powers are too weak
and that the power of God has a force to
spiritually succeed.
I pray that we will continue to know that with
God we gain a peace of mind and
spiritual love for us to employ.
I pray all could experience that consciousness
with our LORD for they would lose that
empty life and live a life of joy.

Hebrews 11:6
But without faith it is impossible to please Him: for he that comes to God must believe that He is———the rewarder———

A Prayer As A Poem — Richard A. Dixon

October 27

Evil And Sin Are Not For The Living Soul

On this day I pray to let the world know
exactly what is the number one bad
thing that destroys the soul.
Evil and sin run together, you do evil you
find yourself in sin, there is no other
way the story can be told.
Many places now you can see the infested
soul, you hear lies, you see fights, and
you smell evil causing crime.
Hatred is running rampage, chaos is the only
thing that is organized, sin is
working double time.
I pray that our people will wake up for this is
not living, this is the walking dead, and instead go with
God and find spiritual love and peace.
Let all pray for His spirit and His strength for
good overcomes evil, go God's way so all of
the torment can finally cease.

Romans 5:12
That as sin has reigned unto death even so might grace
reigned through righteousness unto eternal life———

A Prayer As A Poem — Richard A. Dixon

October 28

Guard Against Forgetting Whom You Are And Where You Are

I pray on this day for my heart and soul and
mind will not stop or hesitate in
retaining His holy word.
I pray much that my mind will never revert
and forget the knowledge and understanding
that I have heard.
In life, sometimes we get lost in the moment in
what we are doing and we respond
hastily in a way that is not you.
Your actions may be accepted as normal or
social but you know in your heart that
you are in the wrong pew.
That is why consistency in praying and caring
for others is a must for it conditions the
mind and fortifies your spiritual bond.
I pray to stay always in the spirit so those
memory voids will never appear, so
God and I can always correspond.

Psalm 34:1
I will bless the LORD at all times: His praise shall continually be in my mouth———

A Prayer As A Poem—Richard A. Dixon

October 29

Accountability, Obligation, And Dependability

On this day I pray that I will keep in mind
the one thing that will bond me to
my needy fellowman.
I must not forget my obligation to those who
could use my help to get them away
from a painful wasteland.
Being accountable to others is that caring
and love that comes from above and it
makes us all better.
It connects us with love, as God would have
us to be as His goal to be a constant
spiritual trendsetter.
Showing others that they can depend on you will
also show them how much you care
for all and not for just some.
I pray that we will all value each other and have
that spiritual love for each other so that
one day we will all become one.

Romans 14:12
So then every one of us shall give account of himself to God———

A Prayer As A Poem — Richard A. Dixon

October 30

Make It Happen

I pray on this day that I will not be one that
will be guilty of habitual inaction or
one that hinders progress.
This has been one of the most popular negatives
that many of us employ and it is a
block to a positive process.
In order to make things happens we cannot
just talk and say we will do it later,
the time is now.
I pray that in our chance to do His good, we
should do it in doing our best by the
sweat of our brow.
I pray not to just think but to do, not to hesitate
but to go, not to defer but to be active
and go through that door.
I pray that God will forever give me that grace
to work for Him when He calls and
when I finish to let me do more.

1 Corinthians 3:14
If any man's work abide which he has built thereupon,
he shall receive a reward———

A Prayer As A Poem — Richard A. Dixon

October 31

Again It's God's Power Not Our Power

On this day I pray again and face the fact
that it is our God Almighty that makes
things right for every one.
The problem is that we depend too much
on our strength, we become losers
before we have even begun.
I pray that we could see our limits in getting
the right things done we could then see
our lives hanging on a thin string.
I pray that we should know that God Almighty
is the power that we should look to, no
matter what the storm may bring.
Let us pray today for all people to put their
cares in God's hands so that they can
receive their spiritual reward.
I pray that we will all see how futile our
efforts were and that we all were saved
by the power of our LORD.

Matthew 6:13
———FOR THINE IS THE KINGDOM, AND THE POWER, AND THE GLORY, FOREVER A-MEN-

A Prayer As A Poem—Richard A. Dixon

November 1

Being God's Servant From Now Until

On this day I pray that I can see myself
as a channel for my LORD to work
through to others.
My task may carry me to undesirable
places but I will fulfill my deed
and go to another.
I will give to all what has been given to me
I will share with them the wonderful
life my God has given me.
I will pass His Spirit on to those I meet and
I will never tire speaking His word to all
ears to help set their hearts free.
Being His channel, I will show others the goodness of God, He brings peace and spiritual
love and ultimate happiness.
I pray to leave nothing out so all will increase
in knowledge of God's purpose so we can
be a part of God's success.

Psalm 100:2
Serve the LORD with gladness: come before His presence———

A Prayer As A Poem — Richard A. Dixon

November 2

There Is No Question That I Am At Peace With My God

I pray on this day to ask myself am I really at
peace with the place and myself
of where I am?
I say that I have never been more certain of
my purpose for God is running
my Life's program.
I only wonder now why did it take me so long
to give myself completely to Him for my
life before had no real direction.
Since my heart has been open so His spirit can
enter, my life is full of His will and ways, I
draw closer to His connection.
I pray now not only to maintain what I am,
I pray to grow and develop more because
to really know God is to grow.
I pray to know all that he will have me to know,
my living with God for eternity will
be my ultimate rainbow.

John 14:27
PEACE I LEAVE WITH YOU, MY PEACE I GIVE
UNTO YOU, NOT AS THE WORLD GIVES
YOU———

A Prayer As A Poem — Richard A. Dixon

November 3

The Words From Him Are Engraved In My Heart

I pray on this day that every word that I speak in
my prayers are so earnest that they
are blessed and ordained.
I pray that my LORD engraved these words in
my heart and that they are there to stay and
spiritually engrained.
I pray that every word that I speak is heard
by every atom in my soul to capture
all of its meaning.
Let every word from my LORD penetrate the
surface of my soul and become a part of
His spiritual cleaning.
Being totally in His spirit that consumes me is
my desire and His ultimate plan, my spirit
joins with the whole.
I pray that the Almighty spirit will consume
us all so that in the eternal all
will become one soul.

1 Peter 1:23
Being born again———by the word of God, which lives
and abide for ever———

A Prayer As A Poem — Richard A. Dixon

November 4

He Took Me Out of The Prison Of Sin

Let me pray on this day that I will not allow
any part of my pride to cause me
not to do it God's way.
There are sometimes these things inside of us
that bring fear to us and instead of
doing we don't or delay.
We must understand as long as we are doing
God's will we should forget about
ourselves and fulfill it.
Be consistently true to God and to yourself no
matter what may be the outcome for you
are with His spirit.
I pray that I will not ever entertain the thought
of not doing my Lord's work because
I'm thinking just of me.
I know I must do what is right by doing His
will, He took me out of the prison of sin
and now my soul is free.

Psalm 107:14
He brought them out of darkness and the shadow of death, and break their bands———

A Prayer As A Poem—Richard A. Dixon

November 5

On That Day And Since That Day

    I pray on this day and give thanks for that day
that I asked my God to change me and
make me a true believer.
On that day I could hear His voice and my soul
seems to have come alive, His spirit made
me feel good as a receiver.
On that day my heart seems to have taken over
my mind and I thought only to do His
will in every way.
On that day although I could not see God,
I could feel His presence just as sure as
the light of the day.
Since that day I have received an abundance
of goodness and it is because God
has since resided in my heart.
I pray for all people to take this path that I
have traveled and invite Him into your soul
so He can give your life a start.

2 Peter 3:8
Be not ignorant of this one thing, that one day with the LORD is as a thousand years———

A Prayer As A Poem — Richard A. Dixon

November 6

My Defense Is My Spiritual Offense

Let me pray on this day to continue to build
a defense around me that will have a
surface that will hold.
I pray that I will employ the entire spiritual
things that will insure my protection that
will be sturdy and bold.
Let my prayers take position right in front of
me so that I can face what evil that may
come my way with its misery.
Let my spiritual love, thoughts, caring
and sharing take their places above, to
both sides and behind me.
I pray that all beneath me will be controlled
by my meditation and communion with Him
and all of this will make me sound.
I pray and know that nothing can harm me now
because where I walk is always on His
glorious and solid ground.

Philippians 2:15
That you may be blameless and harmless————in the midst of a crooked and perverse nation among whom you shine as a light in the world————

A Prayer As A Poem — Richard A. Dixon

November 7

God Makes My House A Home

On this day I pray that God will bless my home,
for your home is an influence in what you do
and where you go.
Having God to live in your home could be
that reason why your life has
that special glow.
Having your Almighty talk to you as you
ponder some family problem could be
your way to resolve.
When your home is blessed, His spirit covers each
room, everyone in the home gets that chance
to spiritually evolve.
I pray that God stays at my resident for He
will protect it whether I am there
or whether I roam.
With all of His goodness that fills the air and
the spiritual love that He gives, makes
our house a home.

Revelation 3:20
BEHOLD I STAND AT THE DOOR, AND KNOCK
IF ANY MAN HEAR MY VOICE, AND OPEN THE
DOOR, I WILL COME IN TO HIM———

A Prayer As A Poem — Richard A. Dixon

November 8

To Be On The Same Page God Is On

I pray on this day to feel how important it
is to be in tune with the spheres
of the heavenly tone.
To be on the same page that God is on means
that you have been blessed to be
placed in His spiritual zone.
Walking His walk and talking His talk could
only mean that you are getting closer
to His image as He has planned.
Spreading His word as His spirit flows through
your spirit will make things better to
see and to follow His command.
I pray that one day we will all be in step in
God's band as we march together for
He knows our battle is won.
As for now, I pray that we will care and share
that spiritual love as God wills us
to be that spiritual one.

Philippians 1:27
———that you stand fast in one spirit, with one mind striving together for the faith of the gospel———

A Prayer As A Poem — Richard A. Dixon

November 9

My Concern About My God Is Absolute

I pray on this day and feel absolutely certain
about my God and that He will give me
strength to get through this day.
God is why I have this positive attitude and
have a drive to respond positively to
the things that pass my way.
I pray to have the assurance that when I pray
my heart is open for Him to fill it with His
spirit for me to do His good.
My God never fails to comfort me in those times
and for Him not to be in my presence
at all times will be an unlikelihood.
I pray and thank my God Almighty for His power
and the goodness that he has shown, it
assures me that He can do all.
All of this gives me that faith that cannot be
broken and I have no fear that God will be
there to pick me up if I do fall.

1John 5:14
And this is the confidence that we have in Him, that if we ask any thing————He hears us————

A Prayer As A Poem — Richard A. Dixon

November 10

It's Our Trust In Each Other That Secures Our Spiritual Mind

Let me pray on this day that on a person to
person basis we communicate
with each with trust.
In trusting we know the possibilities of one
or the other to do wrong then the meeting
becomes a total bust.
I pray to know that God is pleased when we have
that assurance in one another, it shows that
you have confidence in them.
I pray by establishing this positive situation that
we will see the good that all can give and to
this we all can say A-MEN.
In trusting everyone seems to want to do the
right thing and we all pray and
work for a better time.
I believe that if we pray more for each other
that God will increase our faith and
spiritualize our minds.

Psalm 37:40
And the LORD shall help them and deliver them———
and save them because they trust in Him———

A Prayer As A Poem — Richard A. Dixon

November 11

The Church Is God And God Is The Church

I pray on this day that I will not and others
will not lose faith in the church because
of what people do.
I pray that we will understand that the church
is ordained by God and we worship Him
to see us through.
I pray to know the people are only the members
and what they do will only affect them
in their own low tower.
The divine purpose of the church lets us know that
He is indeed our God on His throne and we
delight in His power.
I pray that we will look at the church as our place
of worshiping and praising and to ask for
His blessings for He is eternity.
Let us not be bother by other members to the
point that you dislike the church for God is
the church for you and me.

Acts 2:47
Praising God, and having favor with all of the people,
And the LORD added to the church daily such as should
be save———

A Prayer As A Poem — Richard A. Dixon

November 12

God's Kingdom Will Give Us What The World Could Not

Let me pray on this day for all of us who may
feel that some family member
has mistreated us at times.
People in general do not respond to others as
they should, they pull down when
you want to climb.
We should continue and hope for a better family
relationship, but remember to seek comfort
in God as your spiritual friend.
For His friendship could very well fill in those
empty spaces that your family fails to fill,
He will help you to ascend.
We should pray that sometimes we could find what
is missing here on earth by continuing
in the care of God's grace.
We cannot govern people's ways but we can pray
and depend on our LORD to make His
home our peaceful place.

2 Timothy 4:22
And the LORD shall deliver me from every evil work and will preserve me unto His heavenly kingdom———

A Prayer As A Poem — Richard A. Dixon

November 13

Look Into Your Heart With God And Be You

On this day let me pray that we do not get trapped
in that situation when our peers
want to mold us to be like them.
We must come to those important decisions when
we have grown and develop through experiences
to avoid future mayhem.
Our God can give us that guidance so that we can
learn from all of the factions of the world
and to positively receive.
In acquiring our knowledge through the power
of God, we will be successful because we
will spiritually perceive.
Let us pray to the Almighty and search our hearts
and take the time to listen to our hearts so
we can find that real you.
By keeping it on His path you and everyone will
be proud of all of the wonderful things
that we are destined to do.

Psalm 118:17
I shall not die, but live, and declare the works of the LORD———

A Prayer As A Poem — Richard A. Dixon

November 14

If You Need Help You Will Get That Help From God

Let us pray on this day and remember the
times those things that went very wrong and you
reached out for God's hand.
You prayed and cried out to God for His help and
soon things got clearer, you begin to
perceive His command.
It is good to pray in your darkest hour for if
you are honest in your heart your spirit
cooperates and the good unfolds.
You calm down and you begin to find a resolve
for it all, you start to put things in it proper
place, reason takes control.
I pray and know that I am spiritually stronger
after communion with my LORD, he
strengthens me to be spiritually active.
I pray all to be true in your words to Him and
He will transform your thinking to His
sacred level to spiritually live.

Psalm 121:2
My help comes from the LORD, which made heaven and earth———

A Prayer As A Poem — Richard A. Dixon

November 15

I Pray To Separate My New Life From The Past

On this day I pray not to focus on the things of
the past that I thought then that
they mattered the most.
I pray and thank my God for the things that I
value now, for now they are at the
top of my spiritual post.
I pray not to put in my new life the things that
held me down for their meanings have
been lost with the time.
I pray that the spirit that I carry in my soul
now will be able to help other souls to
live a life that is prime.
I pray to understand that my past has afforded
me so much knowledge in the things
that I should not do.
Now, God is my light and my days and nights
are equally powered by that light, so I
can see things through.

Proverbs 11:18
The wicked works a deceitful work:———him that sows righteousness shall be a sure reward———

A Prayer As A Poem — Richard A. Dixon

November 16

God Has Loved Us From The Beginning

Let me pray on this day that life and
circumstances have not changed
that much over the years.
I pray that we can face those similar problems
and receive His strength to face
them without fear.
Let us pray to do as all spiritual people have
done over the years and that is to
continue to pray.
Let us pray to continue to share with others
and use His spiritual love actively and
put it on display.
God's love has not change over the years, He has
not stopped loving us, although some have
put Him down.
I pray that all of us from all the years will come
together on that day so that all can see His
glorious crown.

Psalm 11:4
The LORD is in His holy temple, the LORD throne is in heaven———

A Prayer As A Poem — Richard A. Dixon

November 17

Let God Guide Us In This World

On this day I pray for those who are finding
it very difficult to live both for the
world and the LORD.
I pray that all will face the fact that you cannot
expect to have a real life of joy and also
expect His reward.
When you put the world in the same position
as God, you will find much trouble because
their purposes clash.
Your heart must be first open to God for by not
receiving the worldly things through Him
expect a backlash.
I pray that all will be given the spirit of
God to balance their life and to receive
what the world can give.
I pray that God will do with me as He plans,
then I will know that my rewards will be
blessed so I can joyfully live.

Psalm 17:5
Hold up my goings in thy path, that my footsteps slip not———

A Prayer As A Poem — Richard A. Dixon

November 18

Each Prayer To My God Is A New And Uplifting Experience

I pray today and thank you my God for the
enthusiasm that you put in my heart in
my communion with you.
I can honestly say that by the time I end my
prayer my energy has rocketed upward and
beyond the sky and the blue.
Each time that I pray it's like a brand new experience
with my LORD, He talks to me and
I talk to Him as His spirit flows.
I can feel soulful power running through my
soul, the more we commune the more He
tells me what I need to know.
Just knowing that I am talking to my God
one on one gives me more strength of
wanting not this prayer to end.
I have a peaceful anxiety of anticipating my
next prayer with Him, talk to Him so
you He can put your life on amend.

James 5:16
————the effectual fervent prayer of a righteous man avails much————

A Prayer As A Poem — Richard A. Dixon

November 19

Let US First Get Closer To God

I pray on this day that we all pray that we will
indeed get closer to God so that we will
get closer to each other.
By trying to get closer to each other first we
might miss the love in our bonding
as sisters and brothers.
So let us pray to get closer to God in every
thing that we do for we want everything
to be ordained by Him.
Let us pray that the bond that we form with
His help will be eternal and will be one
of His spiritual gems.
I pray on this day to do my part as His master
plan is designed to create His universal
collective oneness.
Let us all pray to be a part of His kingdom
and to be glorified with His grace and His
spiritual goodness.

Acts 6:4
But we will give ourselves continually to prayer, and——
——of the word———

A Prayer As A Poem — Richard A. Dixon

November 20

I Wish My Will To Be God's Will

I pray on this day in the form of a wish that if I had
but one wish, I would wish my will to
be as His will in its purest form.
By being so, I will have no reservations about
worry or fears, for its powers will always
walk me through the storm.
I pray constantly now for my will to be
subordinate to His will, but somehow
someway it raises its selfish head.
But thanks to God, although I might be a
little off key, in the end I do commit
to the will of God instead.
I am praying for the strength that will give
me the power to achieve this goal and
climb these hills and slopes.
So I will continue to pray to know that I may
not reach that perfection but the thought
of it gives me eternal hope.

Hebrews 13:21
Make you perfect in every good work to do His will———

A Prayer As A Poem — Richard A. Dixon

November 21

Get Your Life Back On The Track

Let us all pray on this day and see our
reflection and let us look spiritually
at the person that we see.
Do we see a person that is honest, pure in
heart? Do you actually see the person
that you are striving to be?
Take another look at yourself. Do you think
God will be in the least satisfied in
how you are doing His will?
Or do you think God will say to you, "My
child, my child everything that you are
doing is going downhill"?
I pray that we all should be sure about our connection with our Lord for it is never too
late to get your life back on track.
God is good, He knows us all, if you have left
His side God has already put in His plan a
way for you to come back.

Isaiah 57:11
————to revive the spirit of the humble, and to revive the heart of the contrite ones-

A Prayer As A Poem — Richard A. Dixon

November 22

I Pray To Continue This Holy Journey

I pray on this day again to acknowledge the
wonderful things that happen in my
travels as I follow his sacred road.
There is no mistake about how He feels about
us He is always there and welcomes the
chance to carry our heavy load.
The longer or the more I travel his route
the more my spiritual love from Him
flows to other hearts.
The great amount of energy that I receive from
this experience goes far beyond any
of the earthly charts.
I pray to continue this holy journey for it
puts me in the mainstream of my God's
master plan to do my share.
I pray and thank my God for His love and
now as long that I am on his path, I'm
sure he will always be there.

1 Thessalonians 4:12
That you may walk honestly toward them that are without, and you may have lack of nothing———

A Prayer As A Poem — Richard A. Dixon

November 23

Hence To The Wise To Follow His Law

Let me pray on this day and review the principles,
the laws that glorified God's
grace and His spiritual way.
Let it be known that it is a must to follow
His moral rules if you wish to avoid
trouble and individual dismay.
Everything that is organized has rules, God's
rules are divine in purpose and spiritually
motivated with love.
Spiritual love right up to caring and honesty
are the things that should be in your
heart that fit like a glove.
Let us pray to place all of God's ways in our
hearts, let us not be hampered by those
things that will make our soul hollow.
I pray to focus on the commandments handed
down by God that should be our close guidelines
that we should always follow.

Galatians 5:14
For the law is fulfilled in one word————thou Shall love thy neighbor as thyself————

A Prayer As A Poem—Richard A. Dixon

November 24

Do Not Turn Out To Be The Problem

I pray on this day that we again not be
guilty in creating a complexity in a problem
that was not complicated.
I pray not to be responsible for negative
input for it is the positive actions
that should be illustrated.
I pray for the guidance of my LORD that
He will give me the calmness that is
needed to address a wrong.
I will also pray for all concerned that they
will be positive and that their minds
will be spiritually strong.
Let us all take that path of being positive in
our attitudes for by doing things this way
we can all make progress.
I pray that I will not be remiss and keep the
faith and keep Him in my heart so that
our results will be the best.

1 Thessalonians 5:22
Abstain from all appearance of evil———

A Prayer As A Poem — Richard A. Dixon

November 25

You Did It Your Way

On this day I pray to follow the way of Christ
Jesus when He was growing up with His
earth family from day to day.
It is written that he grew up and became a
carpenter and the rest of His family grew
up and did it their way.
Jesus did not try to impose His habits on
His family, this is a lesson to learn, he preferred
that time run it course.
Sometimes some of us have that fantasy thinking
of knowing it all, they should stop
trying to use control and force.
I pray at all times that I will be compassionate
in my responding so that all will know
that I respect who they are.
I pray that all of us will see each other as a part
of a mosaic, we are all different but together
we design a beautiful star.

Job 23:11
My foot has held His step; His way I have kept———

A Prayer As A Poem — Richard A. Dixon

November 26

Your Decisions Make You Or Break You

      Let us pray on this day that we know exactly
          who is responsible for your life in
            how it goes and how it ends.
     We as people too many times blame others
        or other factions and there is more
             that they reprehend.
   Let us pray and know that everything begins
       with you and it ends with you and
           you are at the controls.
   Your God can help you find the right answers
        to give you direction and show you
          how to reach positive goals.
    Pray to know now that the success of your
      life depends on the strength of the bond
         between you and your LORD.
   We should all pray and open our hearts and
     reach out for His hand to receive His
        grace to be in total accord.

Ephesians 1:4
According as He has chosen us in Him before the foundation of the world, that we shall be holy and without blame———

A Prayer As A Poem — Richard A. Dixon

November 27

Giving Thanks Today And Always

On this day I pray and remember some of the
times when God touched me and blessed
me and put me on His riverbank.
Everyone has these moments and somehow
we forget and sometimes we don't but we
fail to stop and give thanks.
I pray that sometimes we will reflect about those
moments when you know that God was
with you and brought you through life.
For we know if it was not for those moments
your life could have taken a turn and
led to much more strife.
Let us pray to know that God is good for He
continues to give us grace although we
might not be quite right in our living.
I pray that we all reach back and reflect
on all of these moments and count our
blessings on this day of thanksgiving.

Psalm 100:4
Enter into the gates with thanksgiving————be thankful
unto Him, and bless His name————

A Prayer As A Poem — Richard A. Dixon

November 28

It Is Good Advise To Use What God Gave You

I pray today to remind myself of the divine
gifts that God has built-in to stay
in our hearts and souls.
Some of us do not even realize that there is
a divine spark of God's spirit that is
part of what makes us whole.
Many of us know that we can think for ourselves
but they do not know that the will
power was given purposely to us.
We should all pray that we should kindle that
spirit and glorify our will power so that we
will become a spiritual plus.
I pray to use my power of choice and ask my
God to come and stay in my heart for His
way is the only way we should go.
I pray that all of us will make the same choice
for then we will get closer to Him and we
will spiritually develop and grow.

Romans 6:23
The wages of sin is death: but the gift of God is eternal life———

A Prayer As A Poem — Richard A. Dixon

November 29

I Pray For All Of My Past, Present, And Future Friends

Let us pray on this day and briefly touch
on the thoughts of the friends that
we had in the past.
Our school days full of young thoughts
about real life, mistakes were made
in our fantasy blast.
Years later, we spent time with friends and
mistakes were made, the full picture of
life was not yet in our heads.
We wonder where are all of those past friends
since we have found God and we put down
the life that we once led.
I pray now for all who have touched my life for
I have to admit that they have been a part
of what I was and what I am.
I pray that somehow they found their real
purpose in life with God for this way they
avoid having a whole life of sham.

Numbers 6:24
The LORD bless you and keep you———

A Prayer As A Poem—Richard A. Dixon

November 30

The Priest Of All Priests

I pray on this day and give thanks to God for
His grace and giving us the Priest of
all priests that walk this land.
Our Christ Jesus' ultimate purpose is known that
He came to die for our sins but He also
reached for our hands.
He came and healed and helped many and
with His divine powers He raised the
dead as part of His work.
Jesus lived His life on earth, He suffered
the pains of life and his feet were also
covered with mud and dirt.
Our Lord Jesus was indeed a rank-and-file Priest,
He walked talked and He listened
to all of the people that he met.
I pray that we will all show our gratitude,
with our thanks and our fulfilling His
way will be gloriously well-kept.

1Timothy 2:5
For there is one God and one mediator between God and men, the man Christ Jesus

A Prayer As A Poem — Richard A. Dixon

December 1

A Prelude To The Real Meaning Of This Month

Let us pray on this day and remind ourselves that this
is the month that has been proclaimed
when Christ was born.
I pray as a Christian that we feel uplifted about
Christ every day and His birth gives
us delight and not to mourn.
At this time of the year there will be many
sideshows that will remind us it is Christmas
but we should focus on Him.
Somewhere along the way, exchanging gifts
has taken over that day and we only see
the shadow of Bethlehem.
I pray that all have joy in their hearts during
this Christmas season for there is caring
for each other at this glorious time.
I pray that we will just take a moment during
this month and remember our savior and
pull the cord that rings His chime.

1.John 5:1
Whosoever believes that Jesus is the Christ is born of God———

A Prayer As A Poem — Richard A. Dixon

December 2

God Is Only Perfect

On this day let us pray not to be so serious
about thinking in terms of this world as
a perfect earth.
My God must direct my thinking on this
perception and I cannot see this world
as perfect worth.
I pray to know that God's plan is already
in place and He has prepared a world
for us in His beyond.
I pray that this is a testing ground for us
to be judged only by God and to see with
Him who will bond.
I pray to know that if we wish to think
perfect we should think of his kingdom
and this is what I believe.
Thinking perfect is thinking God, I pray
for that day to see heaven when all
good hearts will be received.

Psalm 19:7
The law of the LORD is perfect converting the soul———

A Prayer As A Poem — Richard A. Dixon

December 3

Praying Is Not A Habit Or Ritual - It's My Life

I pray on this day that my daily prayers
and my communions are not just a
habit and my heart is not there.
I pray to know that my spirit has awakened
within me and I have been blessed to His
presence and of this I am aware.
My life has been completely gloried by His
spirit and His grace and I will hold onto
this bond come what may.
I treasure with all of my heart every prayer
to Him and every word, and this gets
me through everyday.
I pray to let the world know that this is the
most important part of my life for I
can feel Him securing my goal.
Praying should be a must for everyone for
it is the lifeline, for this is when your
soul talks to His soul.

Psalm 119:105
Thy word is a lamp unto my feet, and a light unto my path———

A Prayer As A Poem—Richard A. Dixon

December 4

Keep Your Spiritual Life If It Means Your Life

On this day let us pray to continue to be
aware of all of the things that will
endanger your spiritual life.
I pray that I will never allow anything or
anybody to come between my God and
I that will bring strife.
I pray to know that the forces of evil could
come from any direction but I will keep
up my spiritual guard.
With God I pray that this is my one priority
in my life and there is nothing
more higher in regard.
I pray and know that my God will be there
for me and I need only to keep the faith so
that He can show me the way.
I pray to know with my trust that He will shield
me with His spirit and then my spirit
will be there to help another day.

Psalm 27:4
One thing that I have desired of the LORD, that will I seek after; that I may dwell in the house of the LORD all of the days of my life———

A Prayer As A Poem — Richard A. Dixon

December 5

Standing Too Long In One Place Will Not Be What To Do

On this day I pray that I will always have
an open heart and mind to learning to
increase my spiritual understanding.
I pray that we should always strive and
thrive to do better for our achievements
should be commanding.
I pray that my steps will be forward to exist
and survive and by standing in one place
will not be the thing to do.
You will either rust out or become immobile
because of inactivity and with these interventions
there will be no revenue.
Praying to reach complete maturity in His
understanding what God wills is my
will and this is all I seek.
Praying and living to be all I can be so I
can receive all that He gives, this is my
way, my spiritual technique.

John 8:31
———if you continue in my word, then you are my disciples indeed———

A Prayer As A Poem — Richard A. Dixon

December 6

Always Remember To Say The Lord's Prayer

On this day let us pray that we will always
include in our praying the prayer
that our Lord gave to us all.
That dynamic energy we get when we say,
"Our Father Which Art In Heaven"
is a glorious greeting call.
Calling on Him as our Father has ordained
us as His children and it is in His prayer
that we give Him praise.
His prayer gives us a choice to do His will,
to forgive and ask for forgiveness and a
guide to follow His ways.
I pray to be there to see His eternal in His
Kingdom and His Power and His Glory
that only he can manifest.
I pray and believe that He wants to give
this to all us when we finish our
spiritual earth conquest.

Luke 11:2
And He said unto them, "When You Pray, Say, Our Father Which Art In Heaven———

A Prayer As A Poem — Richard A. Dixon

December 7

It Is Not The Context Of Your Prayer As It Is the Grace Of God

I pray on this day with the understanding that
some criticize praying at all times, up
and down and inside and out.
There are some that actually do not believe that
there is any influence in praying, they
interject lots of doubt.
I pray and hope that the ones that are praying
will be truthful at least in their hearts
when talking to the LORD.
I pray that all will see it doesn't matter who
says what, it is in the lack of not praying
that you cannot afford.
Pray to know that it is God who determines
what response that is made and not so
much the context of the prayer.
Pray to know that it is not your effort but God's
grace that will improve your life and
take you to a higher layer.

Romans 5:20
——————But where sin abounded, grace did much more abound——————

A Prayer As A Poem — Richard A. Dixon

December 8

May My Path Run Right Into God's Path

Let me pray on this day and think of the kind
of life I am living and the kind of values
that I leave along the way.
I pray that through my experiences I have
brought to light my spiritual virtues for
after I'm gone they will eternally stay.
I pray that my actions will be an example
to some that will lead them down that
road that leads to right.
I pray that I will be an inspiration to others
that will give them direction and will
give them spiritual might.
Let us pray to leave a legacy of goodness
that we have gotten from our LORD and
share it with all that we meet.
I pray to leave a path for others that will lead
directly into God's path and God will be the
first whom they will greet.

Psalm 37:5
Commit your way unto the LORD; trust also in Him; and He shall bring it to pass.

A Prayer As A Poem — Richard A. Dixon

December 9

Keeping His Spirit And Keeping The Faith

I pray on this day to realize that there is
more than just putting your
problem in His hand.
There must be that feeling inside of you of
believing that everything by
Him will be manned.
And you might want to watch those times when
some doubt enters your mind you must stay
in your positive thinking.
The key to success is that in trusting in God
there should be no wavering in
maintaining His spiritual linking.
I will always pray and accept that in this process
of self-control I know that in the end
everything will be all right.
I pray to be steady in my patience and feel
His comforting energy and my problem
will end up in His light.

2 Timothy 4:7
I have fought a good fight————I have kept the faith.

A Prayer As A Poem — Richard A. Dixon

December 10

Keep Trying To Move Forward When Things Get Tough

On this day I pray to focus on what is my real
purpose and what is expected
at the end of my goal.
I will consistently pray to God to give me the
strength to know He is with me and
I will have a stronghold.
I pray that I will diligently address those negatives
that have a tendency to jump up
and out of nowhere.
I pray for His constant energy to flow through
me so that my stable and positive
thinking will be there.
I pray to keep that strong determination
and that feeling of knowing
that I will exceed.
I pray that it will be that unbreakable bond
between my God and I is
why I will succeed.

Matthew 16:19
———AND WHOSOEVER THOU SHALL BIND ON EARTH SHALL BE BOUND IN HEAVEN—

A Prayer As A Poem — Richard A. Dixon

December 11

A Glorious Feeling Sailing On His Spiritual Crest

I pray on this day to be pleasantly amazed on how
much your priorities can change with
your new way of living.
Some of the things you used to love became
ordinary things and you think of God only
in His ways and giving.
For some reason many of the earthly things lose
their luster and you concentrate more
on what comes from the heart.
I pray and thank God for this spiritual satisfaction
that I now get and it is because I
have gotten spiritually smart.
I have no doubts in my mind where these
beautiful changes in my life come from,
it is because I have been blessed.
I pray and thank my God for answering my
prayers and for this glorious feeling in
sailing on His spiritual crest.

John 14:20
AT THAT DAY YOU SHALL KNOW THAT I AM IN
MY FATHER, AND YOU IN ME, AND I IN YOU.

A Prayer As A Poem—Richard A. Dixon

December 12

For Those Who Are Still Finding It Difficult To Find Peace

Let me pray on this day and send up a prayer
for those who are still finding it difficult
to find peace in believing.
I pray for those hearts are still in pain and are
not yet completely open to God and it
is not open to full receiving.
You must understand and let everything go that
bothers you, you must forgive others as
well as forgiving yourself.
God wants you to be open with your pain, by keeping
it inside, it becomes a block to help
you off that lonely shelf.
I pray that you will search your heart and listen
for His kindness and the cry of a loved
one to beckon you home.
Pray to know that God is always with you to
help you find that peace and turn your
life into a beautiful poem.

Ephesians 4:32
And be you kind to one another, tenderhearted, forgiving one another even as God for Christ sake forgiven you———

A Prayer As A Poem — Richard A. Dixon

December 13

My Family And Friends Are A Part Of My Life

On this day I pray to appreciate the fellowship
that I have been able to establish
with my family and friends.
No matter how different we all may be, we will be
there for each other and that means
through thick and thin.
I pray that this bond between us will be strengthened
from day to day for we are
in one spiritual accord.
I pray that when we all come together and our
minds are together that we all be
influenced by our LORD.
We all have experienced life and we all have
tried many to be our friends but
God's plan has selected us.
I pray that God will bless us and may God enrich
our union so that we all will travel together
on His spiritual bus.

1John 4:7
Beloved, let us love one another, for love is of God———

A Prayer As A Poem — Richard A. Dixon

December 14

Being The Children Of Our Heavenly Father We Should Listen

I pray on this day to condition my mind not
to be critical in trying to maintain
my spiritual trust.
In receiving the spirit of our LORD there should
not be any negatives to tarnish or make
an evil crust.
I pray that I will be active in caring and sharing
with gladness in my heart so
my mind will be free.
It is faith and trust that open a way for
our God and His spirit and this is the
spiritual way for me.
It will be advisable for us all to be humble in
accepting God's will to do
as God would do.
Being the children of our heavenly Father, we
should all listen for He will make us
always spiritually true.

Ephesians 6:1
Children obey your parents in the LORD: For this is right———

A Prayer As A Poem — Richard A. Dixon

December 15

My Travel Is Protected By God

On this day let me pray and be thankful that I
can travel anywhere and not be threatened
by the presence of evil.
I pray to have it be known that wherever I walk,
whenever I roam, I will not be a part of any
negative or upheaval.
As I pray I am blessed that God has given me
the strength of goodness to fight all turmoil
that comes my way.
I walk with His shield completely surrounding
me so that none of my being will ever
be disturbed or swayed.
My God is the only one that can give me this
shelter and build His fortress and to cover
me with His spiritual cast.
I pray daily and constant to maintain this powerful
protection and I have the assurance
that it will forever last.

Psalm 23:4
Yea, though I walk through the shadow of death, I will
fear no evil, for thy art with me———

A Prayer As A Poem — Richard A. Dixon

December 16

Because Of His Spirit His Love Flows From One To Another

Let me pray on this day and directly capture
that continuum flow of how God's
spirit changes us all.
It is through the flow of His spirit that God can
pass his love as He did in His followers
like Peter and Paul.
I pray and understand that the spirit my God
gave to me opened my heart to others and
I passed it on to them
God talks to me and I have passed these words
to others and this continuum connects us
to form a sacred gem.
It is the efforts of each individual to insure that
the flow will not be interrupted and to this
I will spiritually do it.
I pray that this is God's way of bonding us as
one and to assure that His love flows always
to be ever in his spirit.

Joel 2:28
And it shall come to pass afterward, that I will pour out my spirit upon all———

A Prayer As A Poem — Richard A. Dixon

December 17

Living Without The Guidance Of God

Let me pray on this day and have more compassion
for those who choose to live without the
guidance of the LORD.
You can exist by not putting your problems in His
hands but you will most likely end up with a
significant amount of discord.
As humans created by God in His image and
given his spirit and seed, He gave us
these for we are His own.
In denying ourselves of living our lives as
God planned it, will relegate ourselves to
mere earthy drones.
I pray to live my life as a spiritual one
guided and control by the Almighty
God to give me tormented release.
I need my God to keep me from evil and for
Him to give me His spirit and love so
that I can live in eternal peace.

Colossians 4:5
Walk in wisdom toward them that are without, redeeming the time———

A Prayer As A Poem—Richard A. Dixon

December 18

I Will Survive With His Spiritual Enhancements

I pray on this day that there may be times when
I may feel the weight of the world almost
unbearably on my back.
I pray that I will keep my spiritual composure for
I know with His help that turmoil will be
returned to its evil rack.
I pray and thank God that I know as long as
I keep my life in His hands He will give me
the strength to survive.
There are times when we all must wait for His
resolve, your place in life and time and His
plan must all coincide.
I pray that in these times of tribulations that I
will call on my Almighty God and patiently
wait for His answer.
Having trust and living with His assurance and
His source of power for these are
His spiritual enhances

Psalm 46:1
God is our refuge and strength, a very present help in trouble———

A Prayer As A Poem — Richard A. Dixon

December 19

Courage And Bravery Is Not All We Need

On this day I pray and see that we should send
up a prayer for those who think that courage
will see them through.
They have that selfish feeling that they have a
power within themselves and can win in
anything they ensue.
I pray that they will know that they have a
false vision that will always lead
them to a dead end.
They face problems without a positive plan,
there is nothing positive they
can comprehend.
I pray that these confused ones will summon
their will power and open their hearts
to trust God of good.
When they do this, their lives will change and
become spiritually guided and life
will be as it should.

1 Timothy 6:12
Fight for the good fight of faith, lay hold on eternal life———

A Prayer As A Poem — Richard A. Dixon

December 20

Pray To Be That Spiritual Gardener

I pray on this day to keep in mind that old
saying that everyone has uttered,
"you reap what you sow".
I pray that everyone will take its meaning to
heart and be that gardener that selects that
which spiritually grows.
I pray that all will be careful to not be negative
in their thinking for it will indeed
show up in their harvest.
Everyone should be cautious of their bad
words for this could determine if the soil
has richness or hardness.
I pray that all will be of good cheer with their
open hearts to receive all of His love,
spirit and His grace.
Pray and cultivate a product that will render
caring, so all will have the energy to
finish their spiritual race.

Galatians 6:7
———for whatsoever a man sow, that shall he also reap———

A Prayer As A Poem — Richard A. Dixon

December 21

It Is Not Our Deed That Will Get Us There

Let us pray on this day and make it unmistakably
clear to all who think they have reached
the acceptance of being good.
Pray to understand that Christ is the only being
that has walked this land and did
everything perfect as it could.
We should pray to find out that it is not what
we do that earns His grace, it is your faith
and trust and its might.
The more our knowledge increases about God
the more we find out about ourselves, we are
not so good and so right.
We should pray that our belief in God has a
bond that cannot be broken and your
trust will always be there.
It is these virtues that God and Christ can work
through you and your salvation can be
forever insured as heirs.

Ephesians 2:8
For by grace you are saved, through faith; and that not yourselves: it is the gift of God———

A Prayer As A Poem — Richard A. Dixon

December 22

Eliminate All Uncertainties And Be Filled With Spirit

Let us pray and look at life and approach it
with the vigor of an attitude and say to
all, "Yes I can"!
I pray that I will be able to eliminate that sense
of wavering in facing life, I need
always a positive plan.
I pray and see now that I should never allow any
anti-action to become a part of my
behavior to perform.
I pray to move forward in good by receiving
it from the Almighty, I will stand on
His sacred platform.
I pray forever that my God will give me His
strength to follow His way so that the
right things are done.
I pray that I will be full of grace and armed
with His spirit so that all of my spiritual
battles will be won.

1 Timothy 2:8
———men pray everywhere, lifting up their holy hands without wrath or doubting———

A Prayer As A Poem — Richard A. Dixon

December 23

God's Goodness Follows Us Until We Use His Goodness To Follow Him

I pray on this day to remind others that from
the very first day God has been in our
presence giving us His grace.
He has followed us throughout and has shown
us many times His goodness as He keeps
up with us in the chase.
I pray and understand that God is our heavenly
Father and He calls to us to open our
hearts so He can come in.
As family he wants to give us his love, His strength,
he wants to make sure our hearts
have a spiritual begin.
I pray and know that He is there when you are in
pain and when your mind is troubled as you
sing that spiritual hymn.
All should know that we all are in His master
plan and His plan will always be to follow
us until we follow Him.

1 Timothy 6:11
but thou, O man of God flee these things and follow after righteousness, godliness, faith, love———

A Prayer As A Poem — Richard A. Dixon

A Prayer As A Poem For Each Day

December 24

Get That Spirit Everyday To Pray

I pray on this day because I feel the love, the
energy, and the necessity to spend some
quality time with Him.
I pray that this is my avenue to travel to gain
my daily strength and to keep my light
of life from going dim.
I pray that we should all realize the power of prayer,
God will always answer those who are honest
in what they say.
If you are one that only prays when you get the
spirit, just remind yourself to feel the spirit
each and every day.
God welcomes all of our prayers whether they
are eloquent in style or as simple
as from a child.
He enjoys the prayers straight off the top and
He delights to hear from those that He hasn't
heard from in a while.

Psalm 55:17
Evening, and morning, and at noon, will I pray———

A Prayer As A Poem — Richard A. Dixon

December 25

God Bless That Day When Christ The Lord Was Born

Let us pray on this day and celebrate spiritually
for this day has been the day
our Christ was born.
This day was the day that God gave us Jesus
and He came as our savior, our hearts
were gloriously adorned.
Our Lord Savior Jesus Christ knew His purpose
on earth and He lived His life teaching, healing
us all along the way.
He came to us as grace from our God to die for
our sins, He gave us new hope for eternal life
being born on that day.
I pray and wish my Lord Jesus a happy birthday
and I praise Him for sacrificing
and dying for our sins.
His birth gave us new life and He gave us
salvation, God blessed this day when
Christ was born in Bethlehem.

Isaiah 9:6
For unto us a child is born unto us given————and His name shall be called wonderful counselor————The Prince of Peace————

A Prayer As A Poem — Richard A. Dixon

December 26

Do Not Fill Your Life With Useless Things

I pray that I will not jam up my life in
seeking those things that end up
as surplus.
To possess those things that have no real
value to you is a drawback to
all of us.
In our prayers we should ask our God to rid
ourselves of being overactive in spending
or buying just to buy.
These useless emotions will only result in
negative ends for the simplest answer to this
dilemma is to simplify.
I will pray daily for the answers, the strength
and the directions to give me my purpose in
life, to reach my spiritual goals.
I pray and pledge not to surround myself with
useless things, I will seek that which came
through God to satisfy my soul.

Proverbs 27:3
A stone is heavy, and the sand is weighty: But a fool's wrath is heavy than them both-

A Prayer As A Poem — Richard A. Dixon

December 27

Just A Prayer And A Thought

Let me pray on this day to think of all of the
people and that I see we are really alike and
just different in our program.
I pray to look them in the eyes and my heart
will see that person is no better or
no less than I am.
I really pray that we could all look at each
other and say to each other that
we all are family.
I really pray that we could find that common
ground to care and live with
all in God's harmony.
I pray that we could all depend on each
other when torment and trouble
attack one or the other.
I pray that we will all jump in to lend a
hand to make things right as
sisters and brothers.

Leviticus 19:18
Thou shall not avenge———but thou shall love thy neighbor as thyself: I am the LORD—

A Prayer As A Poem — Richard A. Dixon

December 28

Lead Me Through The Crossroads Of Life

On this day let me pray that when I come to
those crossroads of life that I will
make the right choice.
I pray that I will carefully look north, east, south,
and west in my effort that I will
hear my God's voice.
I pray that through my spiritual diligence that
I will be given the right directions
to travel on this day.
Each day we go through our test in this world
of trials and that is a reason
not to forget to pray.
I pray and understand that many of the
crossroads lead to the negative things
that are of man's land.
I pray that my faith and trust in God will
continue to be strong to keep it all in
His glorious hands.

Psalm 139:24
―――― and lead me in the way everlasting――――

A Prayer As A Poem—Richard A. Dixon

December 29

Ask Those To Forgive You As God Has Forgiven

I pray on this day to open up my heart to those
times when I did not realize the
makings of my selfish ways.
I know now that back then I might have
said something controlled by my selfishness
and spoiled someone's day.
I pray that God will somehow let those people
know that I am very sorry and I would like
for them to know this.
I pray to God that they have forgiven me as my
God has done for all those negatives that I
now have dismissed.
I pray and thank God for my new life and I
pray for all others to come with me in
the spirit and get aboard.
When we all travel this road we will find peace
and we will receive His grace and many
other spiritual rewards.

Matthew 6:12
And forgive us for our debts as we forgive our debtors———

A Prayer As A Poem — Richard A. Dixon

December 30

Hallelujah! - I Am Home

On this day I pray my God that I am walking
ever closer to your kingdom that is
my ultimate destination.
I pray that my actions and responding to life be
in accordance to your virtues and
spiritual foundation.
I pray God that you will remain in my heart
and soul so that my whole being will
become with you as one.
I pray that my mind will be so spiritualized
that I will be the same person to all
from dawn to dawn.
I pray to be in full bloom with nothing but spiritual
love and goodness flowing through my soul
when I finish my earthly roam.
My God when I walk through your heavenly doors
I will welcome the angels singing and I'll say,
"Halleluiah - I'm home, I'm home.

2Peter 1:1
For so an entrance shall be ministered unto you abundantly into the everlasting kingdom of our LORD and Savior Jesus Christ-

A Prayer As A Poem — Richard A. Dixon

December 31

Thank You My God For This Year

Let us pray on this the last day of the year
with a heart that is grateful for
bringing us through it.
I pray O LORD that you have been more
than kind to give us your grace and
your loving spirit.
I pray and know that without you O LORD
giving me your guidance I would have
turned the wrong way.
I give you all of my faith and trust because I
know that my efforts fell short during
the course of the day.
I pray to let you know my God that I really
love you and this is from every
part of my heart.
I pray that if it is in your plan to give me
another year in doing thy will let me
forever do my part.

Psalm 102:27
———and thy year shall have no end———

A Prayer As A Poem — Richard A. Dixon

LaVergne, TN USA
26 February 2010
174324LV00002B/7/P